A Life on Horseback

the stories of

SPENCER KIMBALL MCLEAN

as told to

CYNTHIA K. MCLEAN

For more information contact:
Cynthia McLean
801–1251 Cardero Street
Vancouver, B.C. V6G 2H9
Canada
prairdog@shaw.ca

Library and Archives Canada Cataloguing in Publication

McLean, Cynthia K., 1950-

A life on horseback : stories of Spencer Kimball McLean / Cynthia K. McLean.

ISBN 0-9780315-0-4

1.. McLean, Spencer Kimball. 2. Horsemen and horsewomen--United States--Biography. 3. Horsemanship--Study and teaching--United States. 4. Horsemanship--Officiating--United States. I. Title.

SF284.52.M28M24 2006 798.2'3'092 C2006-900880-9

Editing: Paper Trail Publishing, npauls@editors.ca
Layout and design: Vancouver Desktop Publishing Centre, www.self-publish.ca
Printed in Canada by Ray Hignell Services Ltd.

To our mothers,

Carola Craig Kimball

and

Spencer Kimball McLean

Watertown, 1931

CONTENTS

The West—Denver, Colorado, 1975–2004

Author's Postscript

AUTHOR'S NOTE

A *Life on Horseback—The Stories of Spencer Kimball McLean* began as a way to keep Mother quiet. After her fall off Sandy in September 1999, she was a miserable patient—both in the hospital and out. To divert her from both the pain and the outrage of badly broken bones at age 78, I began to transcribe her stories. Having had professional experience with taping oral histories, which is very time-consuming, I decided to stick with word-of-mouth. Mother would recount stories; I would write down notes and later put my notes into text. Most of the stories I had heard hundreds of times before—in different contexts, with different audiences, often with different points being made. It was not, therefore, hard to keep her voice: These are definitely *Spencer's* horse and people stories, not mine *about* her.

At the same time, this compilation of Mother's stories is filtered, inevitably, through the lens of my experience as Spencer's Number 1 daughter. My sisters, Woo and Caroline, and my brother, Don, all read drafts of *A Life on Horseback* and made suggestions based on how *they* remembered the events. Each would have framed the stories differently . . . I just happened to be the one who wrote this book. The stories truly belong to us all.

In order to make chronological sense of Spencer's life and stories, a certain amount of research was required. Thank goodness for the Internet and for Mother's large collection of books on General George S. Patton Jr., which was supplemented by two notebooks full of her American Red Cross letters. We also sent a query letter to a

October 1999, Denver

number of her far-flung friends, which resulted in stories and photographs even she didn't remember.

The book languished for several years while I was busy with my life in Vancouver. It was the fall of 2003 when Mother and I decided to proceed, after receiving advice and encouragement from several Denver friends. The manuscript was then written and rewritten through a series of visits in 2004, beginning with the fiftieth anniversary of the founding of the U.S. Pony Club, where Spencer was feted as a *legend.* At the time of Mother's death, in May 2005, *A Life on Horseback* was essentially complete.

This memoir of sorts is very simple. Following her preface, the five people Spencer credits as shaping the person she became lead off. Mother's long-term memory was better than her short-term, with the result the book covers the first twenty-four years of her life more substantially than the following sixty. Her mentors gave her the love, advice and encouragement she needed to excel. She generously gave these gifts back to countless children, horses and adults throughout her life. I commented at the celebration of her life last May that Spencer should be remembered as a flower: not an orchid, not a rose, but a dandelion. Irrepressible, down-to-earth and a colorful disrupter of proper decorum, she sowed seeds of encouragement wherever she went.

Mother was not without her judgments and shadows, but she had a tremendous gift for friendship and was the laughing center of any party or horse event she attended. She had an ability to be fully *present* to both people and animals, in ways that inspired not only trust, but also caring. As a friend recently said wistfully, "We all acted better when Spencer was around. No one was left out. We all had fun."

Spencer's horse and people stories end in August 2004, when she wrote her preface. My reflections "On Being My Mother's Daughter" were written after a three-week visit with her over Christmas 2004.

It is likely that *A Life on Horseback* will disappoint many of Spencer's numerous friends. This is not a video able to capture the facial expressions and dramatic gestures that made her stories so entertaining. Furthermore, not only could all names and photographs and stories *not* be told, but some of what I have included may be plain wrong. I apologize and would love to receive corrections and additions at prairdog@shaw.ca.

I offer these stories as a tribute to a remarkable person and woman, who was also my mother. Preparing the book for publication was not always easy, but spending time with Spencer has always been a pleasure, even in grief.

Cynthia K. McLean
Vancouver, British Columbia
September 2005

Preface

I've had such a wonderful life that at eighty-three I'm about ready to wrap it up and say my farewells. Before I go, however—and at the instigation of my Number 1 daughter, Cynthia—I'd like to share some of my stories with family, friends and colleagues who might like to read about all the fun I've had in this lifetime. These stories are also an opportunity to say a big thank-you to my many two-legged and four-legged friends, living and dead, who supported and accompanied me through the years.

I will begin with my mentors: Carola Craig Kimball, my mother, who taught me right from wrong; Red Hines, an Irish horseman who taught me all I know about horses; Miss Virginia Holt, dean of students at Chatham Hall, who ensured I graduated from high school; Miss Charlotte Noland, head of the Foxcroft School, who turned over her riding department to me; and General George S. Patton Jr.—a true gentleman!—whom I knew as an American Red Cross Clubmobiler during the war in Europe. Not only did they instil in me basic values of honesty, hard work and kindness, but they all—in one way or another—also knew how to have fun themselves and seemed to enjoy my mischief.

The first part of this book tells the story of the first twenty-five years of my life and the five people who meant the most to me. I also recount stories of my many animal friends, who taught me so much about unconditional love, loyalty and trust from the time I was a child. Part Two covers marriage, children and my early involvement in the U.S. Pony Club. Part Three continues my adventures in Colorado and the years of teaching kids, across the country, how to have fun with their ponies. It's been a good ride. I have been blessed.

Spencer K. McLean
Denver, Colorado
August 2004

Mentors

Watertown, New York
1921–1945

ONE

Carola Craig Kimball, Mother

My mother was by far the greatest influence in my life. A soft-spoken disciplinarian, she never lifted her voice but would calmly say "Spencer, please sit beside me for I have something to say to you." These words always put "fear" in me, as I knew she had caught wind of one of my recent escapades.

Carola Craig Kimball, circa 1928

The whole neighborhood knew that when something went wrong, "Little Spencer Kimball" was likely the culprit, so Mother received many phone calls. I had to pay by working for those whom I had offended, in addition to climbing the stairs for Mother's hairbrush . . . I deserved every spanking I got and never held it against Mother. She always warned me first. I just never listened!

To understand the handful I was for Mother, I guess you need to know about some of my pranks. Once, with a collection of knives I kept razor sharp, I had great fun cutting down the neighbors' Monday wash lines, after the fresh clothes had been hung out to dry. Another time, I tied a neighbor's front door to the porch post, stuck a pin in the doorbell (which kept it ringing), then hid in the bushes to watch the frantic homeowners thrashing with the door. Eventually they had to go out the back and come around the front to get the pin out of the doorbell!

Some of my naughtiest tricks involved minor damage, like the time I threw tomatoes at a man's freshly painted white house. He came out with a gun and blasted me with rock-salt pellets, which really stung my tail. Then there was the time I aimed a snowball at a street lamp, missed, and watched it sail through a double-paned window into a nearby house. As a teenager, when I should have known better, I used the brass ball on the flagpole of a neighbor's new dock for target practice, after which I had to climb the pole to replace it. Perhaps my most dangerous trick—and Mother never knew about this one—was when I took a dare to pick up some roadkill with a stick and fling it at a passing car. Well, when the stinky mess wrapped around the driver's face, he came to a screeching stop, jumped from the car and came after us. We escaped down the embankment while he cursed and threw rocks.

I didn't get into all this trouble by myself; I had many "partners in crime." One of my best friends was Bob Farmer, who lived nearby and also went to Henderson Harbor in the summers. One early morning in Henderson, we rowed out to a fancy white yacht, which had moored in the harbor the night before. We really were there only to check it out and say hello to the sailors. But when we came around the stern, the sailors suddenly dumped buckets of garbage on our heads, laughing uproariously. Outraged, Bob and I power-rowed back to the dock and returned with a dozen eggs, which made lovely big yellow splats on white ship and white uniforms alike.

Another good friend was Johnny Northrup. He also had a pony and we rode all over town, even places we shouldn't have. About four one afternoon, we went through a farmer's field onto a private golf course. No one was in sight, so we played cowboys and Indians over the fairways, up and over the greens and through the sand traps. It was great fun, we never saw anyone, and I went home happy . . . until I saw Mother waiting for me on the front porch. Of course she had been called and, in addition to getting a licking with the hairbrush, we had to work at the country club cleaning out the dining room and bar for a month. This dark cloud actually had a silver lining when I realized that every morning I could find coins scattered on the barroom floor, dropped by gamblers at the slot machines the night before. I made good money and Johnny never knew about this until the end of the month.

During the Depression, Johnny and I also used our ponies to make money. We sold their manure to friends for their gardens. We sold second-hand magazines, apples and even pigeons—shot in the old Mullen Street School after it was shut down—as "squabs." Less usefully, we dropped cherry bombs in the sewer, which lifted a manhole cover and car around the corner; and we crouched laughing when Johnny accidentally set a fire beneath his front porch, sending his mother into screams of hysteria.

Being a tomboy, in my early teens I tended to run with the older boys, which meant—of course—*more* trouble. Told to be home by 8:30 p.m., I was always on time until one night some of the boys talked me into breaking the glass on a small red box on the side of a telegraph pole. Little did I know it was a fire alarm. When I turned the key, they then told me to stand by and watch "the fireworks." Sure enough, the police showed up and while the boys all made tracks, I was caught and taken to the county jail. The police called Mother, who told them to keep me overnight and she would pick me up at 8:30 a.m. I was put in a cell by myself and rather enjoyed the food, but when they brought me breakfast the next morning I was in tears. They asked me why and I told them that I wanted to stay, because I knew what awaited me at home—that hairbrush again, plus added chores.

I am embarrassed to say that that same gang of boys persuaded me to lure a rather timid classmate out of her house and around the corner, where they were waiting to pounce. And pounce they did, tying her to a tree and whooping as they pretended to set her on fire! One Halloween we tied her up, left her on a neighbor's front porch, rang the doorbell and hid in the bushes chortling. To our chagrin, the family took her in and fed her treats, while we got none.

I really don't know how Mother survived me and managed to teach me right from wrong in the process. Through all my badness, however, she taught me to be honest, to always tell the truth (if I was caught!) and to never really hurt anyone. In the early 1950s, when I returned to Watertown to show my two oldest children the house I had grown up in, I spotted an old lady rocking on her porch. I slammed on the brakes and jumped out: There sat old Mrs. Payne, looking just as I remembered her when I'd cut down her clothesline and tied her door to the front porch post. She stood and exclaimed, "Why, little Spencer Kimball! I want you to know that this neighborhood hasn't been any fun since you left twenty years ago!"

Mother Growing Up

Mother was born in Philadelphia June 7, 1895. Her mother—Ella Rosamond Spencer Craig—was born in 1865 on the Sandwich Islands. Ella's father, Gustavus Mallory

Spencer, was then the overseer of a Maui sugar plantation and mingled with the Hawaiian royal family at fancy dress balls. Frankly, I think he was a bit of rogue, which might explain some of my "badness"?!

Born in 1826, Great-Grandfather Spencer grew up in Watertown, New York. His father, Dr. Gordon P. Spencer, was a prominent surgeon who served under General Winfield Scott during the War of 1812 at Sackets Harbor, New York. Sometime in the 1850s, Gustavus headed west, perhaps stopping by Spencer, Iowa—a town his younger brother George Eliphaz Spencer had founded in 1859. I don't know when he met Emma Stockwell, his wife, but both Ella and her younger sister Bella spent their childhoods in colonial plantation society surrounded by servants. After sitting out the Civil War on Maui, Gustavus headed back to the States in the mid-1870s and hooked up again with his brother G.E. Spencer, who by this time was a Republican senator from Alabama.

Through his brother's connections, Gustavus became the overseer of several cotton plantations in Mississippi. As carpetbaggers, both brothers made pots of money. In the 1880s Gustavus moved the family up to Philadelphia, probably at the insistence of his wife, who wanted Ella and Bella to make "good marriages." My impression is that although he moved in high society and elite Republican business circles, Great-Grandfather did little more, for the rest of his life, than tell "tall tales" of his planter exploits (which no one else could verify) while eating up the family's savings.

In any case, my Grandmother Ella studied piano and voice and went on to become a prima donna soprano, singing on the legitimate stage in the early 1890s. She married Clark Rankin Craig, a surgeon, whose family was not at all pleased to have a

Ella Rosamond Spencer Craig, prima donna soprano, circa 1898

professional singer in the family. After Mother's birth in 1895, they pressured Ella to give up her career and settle down as a society matron. I suspect she resisted losing her independence, which might have contributed to her early death in 1902 when Mother was only six.

Grandfather Craig remarried, but the "wicked stepmother" had her own daughter and didn't want Mother. So off she went to live with Aunt Mary and Aunt Caroline Craig—my grandfather's spinster sisters—who raised her in Chambersburg, Pennsylvania. She loved them so much that the name on my birth certificate was Mary Caroline Kimball, although this changed to Mary Spencer Kimball when I was baptized.

Carola Craig, Chambersburg, PA, 1915

I never spent much time with my Grandfather Craig, although I remember his huge walrus mustaches, which tickled when he kissed me. I recall better visiting the aunts in the early 1930s with Mother. They lived in a big Victorian brick house on Penn Avenue across from Wilson College, which they divided in half, making some money renting rooms to Craig brothers. Surrounded by big trees, the house had a stable out back where Mother sent me to play when I got underfoot. The staircase was magnificently carved out of mahogany and ran up to a landing where a huge red stained-glass window sparkled on sunny days.

A little dog named Azah was Mother's only pet as a child. She began riding in boarding school, although I think her love of horses came from visiting a Spencer uncle who, after the Civil War, had settled on a farm in Mount Airie, Maryland, and hunted on a mule with ears cut down to look like a horse.

Mother was a brilliant student, but was kicked out of Penn Hall for running along the ridge of one of the big school buildings. (Like mother, like daughter?!) She eventually went to Wilson College, where she studied art.

Mother met Daddy—Henry Joseph Kimball—soon after World War I at a Watertown wedding of one of her Spencer cousins. She married Daddy July 28, 1918, and following my brother Craig, I was born January 28, 1921.

Mother as Horsewoman

When I was growing up, Mother rode daily and was regularly bucked off, breaking both arms at least once. She was a good rider but sometimes not a very "smart" rider, climbing on green horses she'd bought at the Saratoga Sales. By the time I was six, she was putting me on her horses to show prospective buyers how "quiet" they were. Thank goodness for Red Hines, her trainer, who intervened when she wanted to put me up on some of the crazier ones.

Mother liked hunters and jumpers and, after training, put them up for sale. The money she made covered the family's horse expenses and during the Depression helped to put food on the table. Horses also paid for my Chatham Hall tuition in the 1930s. She always insisted on first refusal for any horse she sold; subsequently a number of old horses came home. Mother was also an American Horse Show judge.

In the 1920s, Mother kept her sale horses at Madison Barracks in Sackets Harbor, an army base that was an artillery post with mules and horses. She made a deal with the General that in exchange for horse lodging, she would teach the officers' wives to ride twice a week—to keep them out of trouble and give them an alternative to gossip. I was often around the stables and remember Sergeant Pusey sternly telling the enlisted men "No swearing around the little girl" (me!). Later we hunted with Major Von Holtzendorff's hounds on the bombing range at Camp Drum, when Madison Barracks took the horses up there in the summer. We'd hack up from Watertown, and I remember the horses stepping very carefully around all the live ammunition on the ground. The Major also put me up on a mule, and I've ridden mules periodically ever since.

In 1931, Mother started up the Cold Creek Riding Club on an old dairy farm she'd sweet-talked the farmer into renting for a pittance. She always said she did it to keep the kids (me!) off the streets. We stabled our horses there and in 1932–33 an indoor ring was built. She sold some of her horses to Cold Creek families in quarters—one horse for four children, who would take turns riding and mucking out the stalls.

The Cold Creek Riding Club became a real going concern for both kids and adults. Mother brought in instructors like Captain Von Bretzel, a Russian cavalryman who'd come to the States following World War I. She also put on horse shows with prisoners sprung from the Watertown jail, who set up the jumps and did the heavy work. Never once did she "lose" a prisoner; in fact, the guys competed to join the crew and had as good a time as anyone.

Mother and I went to a lot of horse shows together. I think I won my first trophy in 1929 at the Jefferson County Horse Show, for Children's Jumping. Eventually I had an entire wall full of silver cups and ribbons.

The last time Mother rode was the fall of 1942, when she came to visit me at

Foxcroft. She'd not ridden for several years after a bad fall that broke her back at Henderson Harbor in 1939. To keep her from riding again, I had sold the last of Driftie's foals to a North Carolina man, with all the tack and harness. I therefore tried to dissuade her from getting on one of the Foxcroft horses, but she insisted and promptly fell off at the first jump.

Riders at the Cold Creek Riding Club, circa 1930. Spencer in striped sweater.

On Being My Mother's Daughter

Mother must have been discouraged with me as a "girl," although she never said so. In addition to being a horsewoman, she was a good dressmaker and enjoyed both embroidery and knitting. She made most of my dresses, which I now know were lovely but which at the time—with all the smocking and lace—I hated. She gave me dolls, which I "scalped"; I cringed every time she publicly claimed I was as cute as Shirley Temple (and more talented!); and she mortified me at age seven by tying bows in Tidbit's mane at a horse show. I glumly went to dancing school and then had snowball fights with the boys on the way home.

First grade, 1927

Eventually Mother gave up trying to make me look or act feminine, but she certainly taught me manners and, with her hairbrush, right from wrong. I couldn't go to bed Christmas Day without first writing my thank-you notes. Only once did I ever say a nasty word and immediately had my mouth washed out with soap. And the humiliation, at age six, of having to return and apologize for pocketing a bubble pipe from the dime store cured me of stealing. My brother and I had daily chores, posted on the icebox every week, for which I received an allowance of 25 cents. Ten cents went into my bank account, ten cents into the church plate, and I could spend five cents any way I wished. Mother doted on me, but was determined I would be "properly" brought up and a credit to the family.

The very best thing about Mother was that she loved and accepted me for who I was and placed me in situations where I could excel. I was never much of a student. At about age four I was diagnosed as a "Mirror Reader" (the condition now called dyslexia). But I loved the poems of Eugene Field and had no fear of audiences, so she encouraged me in public speaking. This talent was one of the reasons I was accepted at the Cornell University Agriculture School years later.

One night when I was only four or five, Mother and Daddy were having a party downstairs. My brother Craig and I had been put to bed, but I snuck out and down the hall to his room. I probably was taunting him when he came after me and I fell back through two plate-glass windows, tumbling to the driveway two stories below. My right wrist was shattered and I spent many months, then and later, in hospitals for reconstructive surgery. With a bum arm three inches shorter than the other, there were many things I couldn't do—like competitive swimming. So Mother directed me into fancy diving and one summer, as a teenager, I won a medal in the New York State Diving Championships. Fortunately, my arm wasn't a problem for horseback riding, at which I continued to do very well.

Between my accident and Mirror Reading, I could have been labelled as "backward" but, with Mother behind me, the thought never crossed my mind. She often said "Never lose your pride. Without it you're nothing. And, if you want something badly enough, if it's within reason and if you're willing to work hard, you can do it."

Mother Beyond Horses and Family

I adored Mother and, despite the many spankings, never feared her. But Mother set high standards for both herself and everyone around her, which intimidated many—perhaps adults more than children. She was always fair and treated the jailbirds at her horse shows with as much respect as the society ladies at her bridge parties. If someone, however, had promised to do something and tried to beg off with excuses, she could be glacial. And during the war, when Mother was running the Red Cross in upstate New York, she had no patience for anyone not doing his or her share for the war effort.

During the Depression, "down and out" men often came to our house for a free handout or meal. Mother told me to direct them to our back door, where she would greet them. Always with several cords of wood on hand or a repair in need of doing, she would set them to the task and then invite them into the kitchen for a meal. She always said "You must let people keep their pride, otherwise they will end up as bums and never amount to anything." It was interesting, because some of the men would tell Mother they could get a handout down the street without working, and leave. There were others with pride, however, who came back time after time. They'd do some work, eat a good meal, and after saying "Thanks!" they would leave with a smile.

In addition to her involvement with horses, Mother was a community leader and did all the backroom organizing to get Daddy elected Jefferson County judge in 1934. She had a knack for soliciting donations from her wealthy friends and during the war raised thousands of dollars for the American Red Cross. Neither a prude nor a snob, she happily accepted monies from the madam at the local brothel, despite criticism from some who deemed the money "dirty." In Mother's view, these "ladies of the night" were just doing their bit for the boys in uniform.

Mother could also be quite the wheeler-dealer. She bought an old gristmill in the early 1940s dirt cheap, with proceeds from the sale of some Hawaiian land left to her by her Aunt Bella. Built in the era of the War of 1812, when the American fleet was stationed at Sackets Harbor, the mill was in bad repair and needed a new roof. At this time, both Craig and I were at Cornell, which gave Mother the contacts to invite architecture students up to redo the mill as a "student project." They spent the summer reconstructing the exterior, painting and remodeling the interior, putting on a new roof and clearing the basement of dumptruck loads of accumulated trash, while I spent the summer shooting the rats that lived under all the junk! The Mill became a showpiece and after 1942 was Mother and Daddy's only residence. They spent the winter at the Hotel Woodruff, in downtown Watertown.

The Mill, Sackets Harbor, New York

TWO

TRUE FRIENDS LEAVE FOOTPRINTS ON YOUR HEART

I certainly can't remember all the horses that passed through our hands, but there were favorites which gave me years of fun and adventure. Tidbit was my first pony. Only 10 hands, a tiny Shetland, she trotted me around until I was seven. That summer, at the county fair, I complained that Tidbit was too small and announced I was going to swap her for a brown, 14 hands, two-year-old pony named Chocolate Drop. Mother said, "Okay, but a swap's a swap." As it turned out, the new pony was completely unridable, but that was the end of Tidbit. Eventually I sold Chocolate Drop to Johnny Northrup down the street for $17.50. (Years later, Mother told me she had tracked down the dealer who acquired Tidbit, bought her back and given her to another family. She never let any of her horses drift into the hands of people who might mistreat them or sell them for dog food.)

Trixy was half Arab and half Hackney. Only 13'3", she could jump with the horses and beat out the best at horse shows. She also was a great driving pony. Once at a horse show, an army reservist taught me how to make a horse lie down. So the next day in the backyard, I put a Western saddle on Trixy and tied her front foot to the horn of the saddle. Then I took the far rein and pulled it over the saddle towards me. She ended up not lying down quietly, but falling on me! Of course, I didn't tell Mother what had happened, but during my nightly bath, she noticed all the bruises. When I told her what I'd done, she said, "It serves you right." Another time I was showing off to my "un-horsey" friends and decided to crawl through Trixy's hind legs. She was standing on a slick wood floor and didn't like what was going on, so I was jumped on several times. The result was more bruises and the same response from Mother.

One winter afternoon, I wanted to take my friends for a drive with Trixy attached to a long, low bobsled. Mother was having a bridge party and told me to go ahead and harness Trixy myself; I knew how to do it. So off I went with five pals, all around eleven or twelve years old. We decided it would be great fun to pass by a friend's house where the other kids were ice-skating. But first, we stopped and made snowballs, so when we arrived at the rink and the kids all came over, we pelted them good and made a fast getaway with Trixy.

Being dumb, we decided to try this trick again . . . loaded up with more snowballs and headed back to the rink. Those kids, not being so stupid, were waiting with their own icy snowballs and let us have it! Frightened, Trixy took off at a dead run. I lost one rein, plus the whiffletree of the bobsled hit her hocks as she ran, which scared her more and made her run faster. I yelled for the kids to bail out and since the last turn for home was a blind one, I bailed out too. Trixy was going so fast she didn't make the turn and the bobsled ended up hitting a telegraph pole. It shattered and the last I saw was Trixy galloping off with bits of harness and shafts still attached.

I walked home terrified of Mother's response, especially because I had to break up her card party to tell her what had happened. Mother quietly told me to get a halter and rope and to retrieve Trixy, wherever she had run off to. It was nearly zero degrees, but off I went, following her trail in the snow out of town. The road ran under a railroad bridge and I could see hoof prints going up onto the tracks. Once on the train bed, I could see a freight train stopped about half a mile away, with some men holding onto a very nervous Trixy. Mother arrived about that time and made me lead the pony all the way home. The next afternoon she gave me another harness and told me to train Trixy to accept it. We did get her back in harness, but frankly she never was very dependable after that. After she tipped the cutter over, throwing Mother and a friend into a snowbank, we never drove her again.

After Trixy, I began to ride Robin, who quickly became my favorite. A true friend, he never let me down in the many years I took him for long rides and jumped him in horse shows. He could sail over jumps 6'3" and in 1934 we won the New York State Jumping Championship. Robin was the horse I really learned to ride on.

Robin came to us as an army remount, when he was an unbroken yearling. At that time the army still maintained a cavalry and, to improve the local horse stock, allowed local farmers to breed their mares to the army's top-notch thoroughbred studs for a small fee. Once the offspring were trained, the farmers often sold them back to the army for a good price. But in this case, Robin was mine. Red Hines, Mother's trainer, broke him to saddle and gave him to me to ride when he was about two and a half years old and I was about eleven. I say "ride," but he bucked me off regularly. In fact, it became a game. He'd dump me and then stand there patiently, sometimes nudging me with his nose, as if to say "Hey, lazy girl, get up so we can play again!"

Robin and Bête Noire, circa 1933

Trained to be a jumper, at 15'2", Robin was cat-like and quick. He also was very good-looking, a chestnut with a blaze and two white stockings on his back legs. He moved nicely, had great heart and loved to jump. A playful horse, he was never mean, but I had to watch him or would find myself on the ground again with the wind knocked out of me.

When I went away to Chatham Hall as a fifteen-year-old in 1936, Mother offered to give Robin to the school so that I could keep riding him. But I couldn't bear the idea of sharing Robin and gave him to Harry Bild, a seventeen-year-old boy I had a crush on, who lived in Syracuse, New York. Harry took good care of Robin but jumped him too much—in the ring and out. Robin never stopped and would jump anything he was headed at. He again won the New York State Jumping Championship as a nine-year-old, but within two years had foundered.

Mother brought Robin home the summer of 1937 and we tried to get him going again, but he could hardly walk. Before I left for school in the fall, Mother gave me a choice: She would keep Robin at pasture (he couldn't be ridden) or I could put him down. Many tears were shed, but I knew Robin was unhappy standing around doing nothing, so I fed him his last apple and said good-bye. Mother later gave me a poem about Robin which, in years to come, I always remembered when I had to put down another "old friend." Dozens of nice horses passed through our barns in Watertown, but none captured my heart like Robin.

In addition to Robin, the horses I remember best were Highland Driftwood and Bête Noire. A registered thoroughbred mare and sister of a champion saddle horse that won prizes at the Olympic Games, "Driftie" would lie down beside me and put her head in my lap. Mother schooled her as a hunter, but later sold her to a man at the racetrack as a "running horse." Unfortunately, he mistreated her and said she was crazy. She once ran a race and won, but then threw the jockey and kept running. Mother later gave her to the army reserve to show in Open Jumping classes, but she'd go bonkers. Eventually she came home to us. We bred her a few times and she produced two nice foals.

Daddy rode Bête Noire, who was a character and could do marvellous tricks like turn lights on and off, take cigarettes from people's moths, shake hands and nod his head yes or no. I showed him as a hunter jumper, but later a rich woman paid a handsome price for him and annually took him by boat to England for foxhunting. When she broke her neck falling off Bête Noire, he was sent back to Watertown by boxcar. I skipped school to go with Mother to pick him up at the train station. Bête Noire was so excited to be home that he tried to climb on the running board of the car. When that didn't work, he followed Mother through the middle of town whinnying behind the car, dragging me behind barely able to hold onto his halter. Don't listen to people who think horses are dumb. Bête Noire proved to me they can have great memories.

Highland Driftwood (Driftie), circa 1932

Animals in the House

In addition to the horses, many other animals came to live with us. Mother always said I could have any animal I liked, as long as I took care of it.

White Rock, "Whitey," was an English bull terrier—my constant companion and guardian from the time of my birth until I was ten. Mother could let me go outdoors and not worry, knowing that Whitey would keep me out of the street by holding onto my clothes. She also was the only dog allowed in the Mullen Street School, just around the corner from our house. She'd take me over in the morning, lie quietly under my desk during school hours and then bring me home.

Whitey was a good dog, but when she did get into trouble, it was usually my fault. A bunch of tough boys used to hang out on a corner two blocks down the street. I'd call them names and when they started to come at me, I'd "sic" Whitey on them and she'd attack fiercely. Several times the police came to the house with reports of kids being bitten. But Whitey loved the police; she'd lick their hands, smile at them and wag her tail. Between Whitey's "friendliness" and my tears, Whitey was never taken away. Mother later told me she had had to pay over $2500 for doctor bills and clothing that Whitey had torn.

White Rock was *my* dog and no one was allowed to hurt me. Daddy and I had a game where he, who never ever disciplined me, would in a loud voice pretend to grab and hit me. Whitey would immediately jump between us, growl at Daddy and show her teeth. I do believe if Daddy had kept it up, White Rock would have attacked.

Whitey was very protective of her turf; the only other dog she would tolerate was a mixed male pointer that stayed with us for a year. His name was Blotto and he carried a rock around in his mouth the whole time. Blotto loved the water. I could throw a large rock off the end of the dock and Blotto would jump in, swim to the bottom and come up with a large rock—not necessarily the one I had tossed in. He also, if not locked up in the house, would swim after our boat—no matter the distance—when Daddy and I went fishing. I had to plead with Daddy several times to turn around and pick him up, because I was afraid he would drown trying to swim across Henderson Harbor.

When Whitey was put to sleep at age ten, Red Hines brought me a Dalmatian puppy called Freckles. A nice dog, but no Whitey, Freckles became a "beggar" and spent her days going downtown to get free handouts from the butcher shops. When Mother and Daddy were at the Mill in Sackets Harbor during the 1940s, she would slip through the guard gates at Madison Barracks to make the rounds of the army kitchens. Needless to say, she was always too fat. Unlike Blotto, Freckles also hated the water. When she was a puppy, I thought that all dogs knew how to swim, so I tossed her off the dock at the Clayton Yacht Club and she immediately sank to the bottom. I had to jump in with all my clothes on to save her and it was a very cold, blustery day in May!

Freckles lived with us until I came back from Europe in 1945, where I'd been with General Patton's Third Army. She was old, old, old and I had her put to sleep.

As for other animals I enjoyed—when I was five or six, I made friends with a mother skunk that lived under our barn. Once, when Mother had "something to tell me" (I'd been bad again), I hid out with Mother Skunk under the barn. When Mother got down on her knees and peered in, trying to find me, Mother Skunk marched right to the entrance and backed towards Mother with her tail in the air. Mother retreated quickly! Mother Skunk let me play with her babies. When she disappeared two years later, I was heartbroken.

White Rock and Craig (brother), circa 1925

I had guinea pigs, which I liked better than white mice, because they talked to me when I came near their cage. For a short time I also had a white rat, which my older brother Craig put into a glass milk bottle one day. The rat slipped in okay, but was too big to turn around and get out. I cried and cried until Mother, by carefully breaking the bottle with a hammer, saved him.

Red Hines brought me a snowy white owl we named Whosis, and I also had a yellow canary called Peep. I'd let Peep loose in the house and he would head straight for the sideboard in the dining room, where he would sing and strut up and down, admiring himself in the polished silver. Mother got him a mate that hatched out babies, which were immediately pushed out of the nest onto the floor, where they died. When the next batch hatched, I was able to save two of the chicks. We put them in a cotton nest on the warmer over the wood stove and I fed them with an eyedropper.

The two rabbits we had weren't very interesting; they only ate and wiggled their noses. Coonie, a racoon Red brought me, was great fun, but caused havoc in the kitchen by opening up the cupboards, unscrewing the tops of jars and tossing preserves all over the floor. When he was older, we turned him loose. He stuck around for a few weeks looking for handouts and then disappeared.

I sure was lucky to grow up with so many animal friends, not least after "hairbrush episodes" when I was sent to my room to contemplate my "badness." My pets always listened sympathetically to my tales of woe—and didn't talk back.

THREE

WATERTOWN, DADDY AND FAMILY

In retrospect, Watertown was a wonderful place to grow up. The principal city in northwest New York State from the early 1800s, the city was laid out alongside the falls of the Black River, which provided power for paper and pulp mills and cotton and wool manufacturing factories. These industries drew thousands of Irish and Italian immigrants in the late nineteenth century, who lived in the "Flats" down near the mills. The Black River emptied into Lake Ontario through Black River Bay; the river was full of limestone caves which once had been used for smuggling rum and guns, as well as runaway slaves coming through on the Underground Railroad during the Civil War. I loved exploring these caves with my pals when Mother wasn't looking; she had told me they were strictly "off limits."

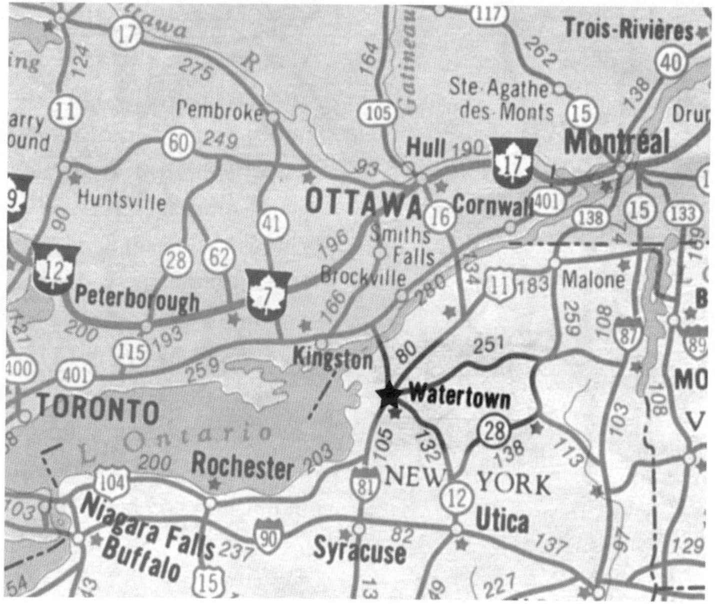

Waterton and surrounding area.

Thirty miles from the Canadian border, Watertown early on became a supply depot for several military installations. During the War of 1812, the U.S. Navy stationed its Great Lakes fleet at Sackets Harbor, a major shipbuilding center at the entrance of Black River Bay. When General Zebulon Pike (of Colorado Pike's Peak fame) was killed at the Battle of York (Toronto) in 1814, it was to Sackets Harbor that they shipped his body in a rum barrel. Fort Pike later became the more substantial Madison Barracks, where the army trained officers who went off to Cuba and the Philippines in 1898 and to China during the 1901 Boxer Rebellion. Madison Barracks was flourishing when Mother and Daddy refurbished the Mill. After World War II it was abandoned, turning Sackets Harbor into a near ghost town for several decades.

Northeast of Watertown, the army in 1908 requisitioned several thousand acres for Pine Camp, later called Camp Drum. In 1936 the largest peacetime military maneuvers in U.S. history were held there, and during World War II, college boys in the Reserve Officer Training Corps (ROTC) came to learn artillery skills. That's where I met Don, my husband-to-be, in 1941.

As a child, I took this military presence for granted, but I realize now that it significantly shaped my respect for horses as "working animals." Only in the 1930s did the army phase out horses and mules, replacing them with trucks and tanks. I do believe that if I'd been born a boy a generation earlier, I'd have joined the U.S. Cavalry.

HENRY JOSEPH KIMBALL, DADDY

Henry Joseph Kimball was born November 18, 1889. His great-grandfather, Crafts P. Kimball, was a country doctor and homesteaded in Burrs Mill, just southeast of Watertown, in 1808. The horse artist Sam Savitt later drew a picture of the sleeping doctor on his steady horse Jenny. Like Mother's great-grandfather—Dr. Gordon P. Spencer—he too served as an army surgeon during the War of 1812. Some years later, Crafts Kimball built a great stone house and bought a small herd of cows which his son, Henry N. Kimball, developed into a prosperous dairy farm. The farm was then passed on to Frederick H. Kimball, Daddy's father, who married Mary Ann Jones—beauty queen of the Jefferson County Fair—in 1888. Unfortunately, addicted to betting on trotting horse races, Fred H. lost the farm to creditors and in 1896 moved the entire family to Watertown, where he worked the rest of his life for the coal company.

Daddy went through high school in Watertown and was the first in his family to go to college. He went off to Cornell University with $17 in his pocket and worked his way through by waiting tables in a fraternity house. Class of 1911, he also was the coxswain on the unbeaten Cornell crew, which won the Varsity Eights at the intercollegiate regatta the year he graduated. After Cornell, Daddy attended law school for a year and passed the state bar examinations in 1913. One of the first in Watertown to volunteer for service in World War I, he was commissioned as a second lieutenant and later a captain

Dr. Crafts P. Kimball and Jenny (drawing by Sam Savitt, 1974)

of infantry, but was then transferred to the army's judge advocate's department at Camp Dix, New Jersey. He married Mother the summer of 1918 and had a private law practice in Watertown when I was born in 1921. During the Depression, he took a job in a bank.

With Daddy, Mother and Craig, 1921

Daddy always held me in his arms when I was hurt, bad or frightened. He was a very kind person and I could wrap him around my little finger. I'd climb into his lap and could get him to do most anything I wanted. He tried so hard to teach me Latin—it was a lost cause, but I always enjoyed his company. We spent the summers at Henderson Harbor during the 1930s; Daddy would come home from work and I'd take him out in our rowboat to fish, with the "night crawlers" I'd dug for bait. We spent many, many hours together—just the two of us.

Less down-to-earth than Mother, Daddy had few mechanical or "handy" skills. He'd drive his car with a flat tire until he found someone to fix it. He painted the bus stop outside the Mill and came home with more paint on him than on the shelter. When he could not put together twin beds bought for the Mill, he went for an axe. In this case, Mother and I intervened, locked him out of the room and put the beds together ourselves. Once he scared me. A staunch Republican, he swore he'd shoot himself if Roosevelt were elected in 1933. The night Roosevelt was indeed elected, I heard a gunshot and hid under my covers, certain he'd done it. But when I came downstairs the next morning, I discovered a gaping hole in the living-room ceiling: He had been cleaning his gun for duck hunting when it misfired, with the bullet going right through the floor!

Mother was the disciplinarian while Daddy was just the opposite. A gentle soul, he wasn't really ambitious, although he had participated in local Republican political circles since college. I think it was Mother who got him elected Jefferson County judge in 1930. In 1938 he resigned to become the Republican nominee for a New York State Supreme Court vacancy. He won and spent the next twenty years on the bench of the appellate division. As it turned out, he was a very good judge, respected for his fairness by all—even the criminals he sent to prison. When I was with the Red Cross during the war, I met a young soldier who had stood before Daddy in court. The soldier wouldn't tell me his crime, but had nothing but good things to say about Judge Kimball.

Watertown Family

We gathered as a family once a week, usually for a meal. This mostly involved Daddy's family, the Kimballs, but Spencer relatives showed up periodically too. We had a lot of fun with charades and dictionary games, playing rummy and even poker, putting jigsaw puzzles together and singing. Outside, we kids also played hide-and-seek, kick the can and king of the castle. No radios, no television, no videos, no computers—we created our own worlds of play and mischief.

I had only one cousin, Bruce Otis, while growing up. (Daddy's brother Fred and my Aunt Alda produced cousin Hubert when I was twenty-one.) Bruce's mother was Daddy's sister, my Aunt Jessie. Bruce was in my class at school and I was closer to him than to my brother Craig, who because of his asthma, tended to stay indoors more. Bruce ran with all the kids but managed to stay out of trouble (unlike me!). One afternoon, when I was walking home with Bruce, he informed me that there was no such thing as Santa Claus. I had a fistfight with him, shouting, "My mother would have told me if there wasn't a Santa Claus. You're a liar!" I hurried home crying and told Mother what Bruce had said. Very quietly she said, yes, there *is* a "Santa Claus"—herself and Daddy. That suited me just fine.

Grandfather and Grandmother Kimball, Bruce (cousin), Craig and Daddy, 1935

Aunt Jessie and Uncle Dave Otis were wonderful people. They lived just around the corner from us in Watertown, in a two-family house built by one of Watertown's first settlers between 1823 and 1826. Situated on a street corner, the house had two distinct entrances, but shared a basement where I could race back and forth visiting Grandfather and Grandmother Kimball, who lived in the other half. Aunt Jessie and Uncle Dave spent their summers in Cape Vincent, New York, about thirty miles from Watertown on the St. Lawrence River. The Cape house, which had been in Uncle Dave's family for generations, was built around 1815 for Napoleon's officers, who had expected Napoleon to escape Elba and join them there. The French influence was obvious both in the architecture and the fifteen-foot ceiling in the living room, which was constructed around nine oil paintings of Napoleon, Lafayette and Chateaubriand peeking out through the clouds! Uncle Dave's eyes had been damaged by mustard gas in the First World

War, but he was a talented gardener, and we spent many summer afternoons playing croquet among all his beautiful flowers

I also loved Grandmother and Grandfather Kimball very much. One Christmas morning, when I was a little girl and still believed in Santa, Grandfather led me behind the house to show me where Santa and his reindeer had landed the sleigh. (Our house had no chimney or fireplace.) There in the snow were runner tracks and deer footprints! I was enchanted, even years later when I discovered Grandfather had made the tracks himself by fashioning a hoof to a stick and stamping the snow. A soft-spoken man, he seemed to enjoy all my pranks. When I was a little older, I often took Grandfather for rides in the cutter with my pony.

Sometime in the 1930s, Mother rescued my Grandmother Ella's sister—Bella Spencer Champeny—who had been living in not so genteel poverty in Philadelphia. She had married an Episcopal minister who ran out on her, but always remained devoted to the Church and had a "special feeling" for all creatures great and small. This became something of a problem when one day she found Mother sweeping all the spider webs out of the barn with a big broom. The next thing we knew, Aunt Bella was trying—by hand—to pluck entire spider webs out of the barn to place on the grass, where the spiders would at least have a chance. Aunt Bella also boycotted Sunday dinners for a while when she discovered that the delicious "chicken stew" she'd been eating was actually a rabbit that my brother had shot in the woods. Auntie lived with us for about five years; I just wish I had asked her more about her memories of Hawaii and her sister, my Grandmother Ella. She brought with her a huge steamer

Alf Gillett and Judge Henry J. Kimball

trunk, full of fancy ball dresses, feather fans and photos of the king and queen of Hawaii in royal dress.

Aunt Bella died in 1939. Mother sent her body by train to be buried in the Spencer family plot in Philadelphia; unfortunately, the coffin was never unloaded in Philadelphia and went all the way to Florida. It took Mother weeks to sort out that snafu.

Not a blood relative, but definitely a member of the family, Alf Gillet was an Englishman who came to the States as a groom for a wealthy English family. Landing in Boston about 1915, he worked his way west, finally showing up at Madison Barracks, where Mother hired him in the late twenties. Alf was a good horseman and served as a butler at Mother's many cocktail parties (she never touched a drop). Later he became a brilliant gardener when they bought the Mill at Sackets Harbor. Alf, however, also enjoyed his whiskey and to Mother's utter frustration continued to drink to excess through the many years he lived with us. Mother regularly threatened to fire him and once locked him in his room for three days to "dry out." It didn't work, but he never left.

When I went to England with the Red Cross in 1944, I looked up Alf's relatives—aunties and cousins—who were delighted to hear stories of "little Alfie," who had left the U.K. so many years before. I last saw Alf in 1957 at our farm in Manlius, New York, when we were packing to move to Kentucky. He never mentioned it but must have had trouble eating for a while, because the movers packed his false teeth, which we found only months later. Alf died of a heart attack at the Mill on Christmas morning 1958.

FOUR

Red Hines, Miss Holt and Miss Charlotte

Red Hines was my first best buddy and, after Mother, my second mentor in life. Mother met this Irish trotting-horse man at the racetrack in the late twenties and soon hired him to help train the green horses she was buying for sale. Thank goodness for Red, who saved me from Mother many a time. If I was bucked off one of her young horses more than twice, he would intervene.

My first clear memory of Red was the day he brought me a snowy owl we named Whosis. I loved that little creature, which ate the mice in the barn behind our house. But he had lived with us just over a year when I found him one winter morning frozen in a heap on the barn floor. I put him near the furnace to warm up, but he was already dead. Red took Whosis away and some weeks later when I walked into the house I spotted another snowy owl perched on the living-room mantel. I was so excited; Red had found me a new Whosis! As it turned out, however, it was the old Whosis—stuffed. I howled. I didn't want a dead Whosis in the house! Red carted him off.

Around 1929, Red essentially became my "babysitter" while Mother took my brother

Craig to see asthma specialists in New York City and South Carolina, sometimes for months at a time. I was hurt that Craig seemed to be going to exciting places while I was left at home, but Red kept me busy and taught me most of what I know about horses.

Incredibly patient, Red could teach anything to anyone, four-legged or two-legged. He seemed to communicate by telepathy; today I think he would be called a horse-whisperer. Red never raised his voice and rarely used a whip, but the craziest horses would stand quietly for him. I remember watching him once enter a corral with an unbroken colt that had worked itself into a frenzy and was frothing at the mouth. Red took a few steps towards the colt and then just stood there for the better part of an hour. Catching the horse's eye, he then took a few more steps forward. By the end of the day Red had a halter on the colt and was able to lead him back to the stable.

Gentle as he was, however, Red also knew how to cure horses of bad habits. I once had a horse that kept rearing and dumping me in the dirt. Red boosted me back up, gave me a bottle of warm water, and instructed me to hit the horse between the ears when it reared. I did and, sure enough, the horse thought the warm water was blood and was so scared that it never reared again.

When I was about nine, Red taught me how to drive a two-wheeled cart attached to a trotting horse at the track. He sent me off at a fast clip, which I thoroughly enjoyed, until I realized that he had neglected to tell me how to stop the horse. Around and around I went, hauling on the reins and screaming bloody murder, while Red just stood there smiling. Finally he told me to ease up on the reins, to let the horse go, and it would stop. It did.

A few years later, soon after I had begun to ride Robin—my favorite horse—Red persuaded me to enter him in a Handy Hunter class at a horse show. I agreed, not knowing that Red had already taught Robin a variety of tricks. The class involved opening and closing gates, jumping in and out of a water jump and stopping on a dime. I discovered that I was a mere passenger on Robin, who did all the work without any direction from me. The spectators quickly realized this too and began to laugh. I was so embarrassed and so mad at Red but had no sympathy from Mother, who told me to cry in the barn until I could come out with a smile on my face.

Lord Bob, under the supervision of Red Hines, 1930

Once Red took me down to see the Ringling Brothers Circus unload and set up. We watched the elephants helping to raise the huge tents, while the other animals were tethered around on the grass. Red noticed a two-humped camel lying down chewing its cud and said, "Hey Spencer, I bet you wouldn't dare climb on that camel!" Of course I did, the camel stood up, and immediately half a dozen roustabouts swarmed me, cursing loudly. Snatched off the camel, I stamped back to Red and said, "Why didn't you save me?!" His soft reply was "I'm just teaching you not to do or believe everything your friends say."

My world broadened with Red, who took me to cockfights and boxing tournaments. I didn't much like the cockfights but did learn to box, which came in handy as I grew older. It was fun to meet Red's friends at the fairgrounds; they trusted him so much that they were willing to sit on chairs and be "jumps" for the horses he was training. It was there too that I met Skippy, a dumb beagle that was constantly getting underfoot and causing confusion. Red taught him to climb a ladder to the top of the horse shed, intentionally not teaching him how to climb down. As a result, Skippy spent many hours howling on the rooftop, until the horses had been put away and everyone had gone home. Then Red would climb up and fetch him down.

Red never spoke of his family in Ireland. He lived quietly at Watertown's "house of ill repute" with the ladies who so generously gave Mother money for the Red Cross during the war. I visited him there frequently, which was never a problem for either Mother or Daddy. In the 1940s, however, Daddy was given a car with JSC—Justice of the Supreme Court—license plates. Following several irate phone calls from "concerned citizens," who had seen his car in front of the "cat house," he asked me to *please* park his car around the back when I went to visit.

I last saw Red soon after I returned home from Europe in 1945. In hospital, he smiled and said that although he was ready to go, he wished he could live just a little bit longer—to train one last horse for me.

Virginia Holt, Dean of Students, Chatham Hall

I went to high school at Chatham Hall in Chatham, Virginia, from 1936 to 1940. Established in 1894 as the Chatham Episcopal Female Institute, it offered a "classical education at minimum cost" and based its curriculum on the entrance requirements for Wellesley College. I picked Chatham because it was in the country and had a good riding program. I spent four wonderful years there.

Dr. Edmund Lee was the head of the school. An Episcopal minister, he and his wife had lived more than twenty-five years as missionaries in China before coming to Chatham. Dr. Lee always needed money for the school, and I can still see him with his hands raised to the heavens pleading "We need this or that, surely the Good Lord will provide!" Amazingly enough, the money always seemed to come.

Mr. Brush was both the school's treasurer and the head of the riding department. He took us on moonlight rides, picnics and all-day cross-country rides; he also taught us to joust. During May Revels, as knights on horseback, we competed to see who could pluck the most rings hanging from a tree with the tips of our lances.

I spent a lot of time with Mr. Brush, not only because of all the fun we had with the horses, but also because I was frequently "campused" for various infractions of the rules. This meant I couldn't go into town on the weekends, but riding with Mr. Brush was okay.

Mother sent horses to Chatham to pay for my tuition, and when I graduated Mr. Brush and Dr. Lee presented me with a check for $900. They said Mother had overpaid. I donated the money back to the school in Mother's memory.

Miss Virginia Holt was the dean of students at Chatham Hall and my third mentor. She was a severe-looking person who scared me at first, but I found that she had a good sense of humor and fun. That was fortunate, since I again got into all kinds of trouble.

Miss Virginia Holt, dean of students, Chatham Hall, circa 1940

Students with good grades were allowed to study in their rooms at night, while students with poor grades (including me *all* the time) had to report to study hall. I tried to pay attention to my homework, but would get bored and dream up some foolishness, which almost inevitably landed me in the bad books of the teacher in charge. One night, as I sat at my desk, I pulled several long hairs from my head. I tied them together and at one end attached a tiny piece of white tissue paper. At the other end, I gently made a loop, which I then tied around the neck of a huge fly I had caught. When I let the fly go, that little piece of tissue paper fluttered all over the study hall, to the great merriment and laughter of my friends. This so frightened the teacher that she reached for the telephone to call for help. Campused again!

My worse prank, which involved Miss Holt directly, was when I took a dare to enter her private quarters with a tube of liquid glue that we used in art classes. I spread the glue all over her toilet seat and snuck out. The next day at morning assembly, she announced that *someone* had come into her rooms and *done something*. The culprit knew who she was, she continued, and Miss Holt expected her to come to see her immediately. I slunk into her office hanging my head, petrified that I would be kicked out. She looked sternly across her desk at me and said, "I figured it was you." And then, with eyes twinkling, she smiled and added, "I just wanted you to know it worked!"

Miss Holt tried to teach me Latin and English in her free time; this wasn't a great success, but she was determined I would graduate from high school and never gave up on me. I did do well in some classes. I loved the Bible teacher, Miss Thompson, and even won a prize for the best essay on "Who Do You Think God Is?" I wrote about God being in all the animals and plant life on earth. I still feel this way; maybe I was once an American Indian?

Despite all my mischief—and because Mother had taught me to always be truthful—I lasted four years at Chatham. I was a member of the drama club and athletic council, in addition to becoming head of the Riding Club and a student council member. In the spring of 1940 I graduated and received not only a diploma but also the Rector's Medal, awarded to the senior who best exemplified the spirit of the school. I couldn't have done it without Miss Holt.

Mother was the first in life to guide me. Red Hines was the second and Miss Holt was the third. I have always felt badly that I didn't name one of my daughters Virginia after her. Years later, in one of the last photos of Miss Holt in the Chatham Hall alumnae magazine, you can see behind her a framed Christmas photograph of me with my family.

Cornell, 1940–1942

When I couldn't get into Vassar as Mother was hoping (Faint hope! Dr. Lee had already told her I wasn't "college material"), she lined me up to work as a nurse's aide in the Watertown Hospital. But I checked around and found that I might be able to enter Cornell University in a special agricultural program, set up specifically for New York State farm kids. So off I went to Ithaca, New York, and took their entrance exams, which included being able to do public speaking (which I was good at); knowing the difference between various kinds of animal feed; and being able to harness a horse properly. I passed with flying colors and didn't even have to take a remedial English course!

Cornell was great fun, beginning with being assigned a male roommate and a suite of rooms that boasted its own fireplace. I had applied as "Spencer" Kimball and the admissions office thought I was a boy. Mother quickly put the kibosh on that adventure, and I ended up in a stuffy little room near the Veterinary School.

I actually considered becoming a vet, but after watching a piece-by-piece dissection of a horse one night, I lost all desire. I'd simply had too many "pets" and couldn't imagine cutting and slicing them.

My brother Craig was already at Cornell when I arrived the fall of 1940. He protectively supplied me with dates from his fraternity house to keep an eye on me, which I didn't always appreciate. My first year I was actually on the dean's list; this pleased both Mother and Daddy enormously. My second year, however, the war was on and all the boys were leaving to go overseas. I guess I spent more time saying good-bye and partying than I did studying, and in June 1942 the college asked me to leave.

Charlotte Haxall Noland, Foxcroft School

Since I was no longer at Cornell, Mother immediately signed me up again as a nurse's aide. I worked from six in the morning until five at night. I actually loved the work and ended up in surgery, where the doctors taught me how to sew up a patient after an operation. Only six months after the Japanese attack on Pearl Harbor, they felt that if the war came to the U.S., doctors would need all the help they could get.

Then an amazing thing happened in early September. Out of the blue, I had a phone call from Miss Charlotte H. Noland, the founder and head mistress of the Foxcroft School for girls in Middleburg, Virginia. She had spoken with Dr. Lee at Chatham Hall, who I guess gave me a good recommendation, because she invited me down to New York City for an interview. It seems the former head of the riding department had broken her back over the summer and the school needed someone immediately. With Mother's prodding, I met Miss Charlotte and was hired on the spot. I arrived in Middleburg in October 1942 and spent the next two years as head of her riding department. This included the works—teaching, hiring, managing the stable and paying the bills.

Miss Charlotte became my fourth mentor. She was a wiry gal in her sixties, and I admired her guts and determination. We became good friends and she often invited me over to her house for a drink. Quite the storyteller, she told me that during the Civil War, her family's plantation in Middleburg had been overrun and ransacked by Northern troops. Utterly demoralized, her relatives had lost the land, ending up as near sharecroppers. Miss Charlotte was bitter about this and became intent upon restoring the family name. Although she grew up comfortably and was even a debutante, she told me she had left home in her teens and become a circus performer, doing ballerina tricks on horseback! Later she took a job teaching riding at a prominent girls' boarding school in the North. In 1914, at the age of thirty-one, she returned to Virginia determined to buy back the old homestead and get revenge on the North by creating the very best and most expensive girls' boarding school in the country. She succeeded, and Foxcroft today continues her legacy of excellence.

Like my mother, Miss Charlotte was a taskmaster and expected her girls not only to excel academically, but also to be a credit to their communities after they graduated. She set high standards of moral character, leadership and service. With the war on, she removed the linen tablecloths and candles from the dining room, forbade silk stockings and rationed butter. The entire school was put into uniform and taught to drill with wooden guns, like the WACs she had seen in training. When Miss Charlotte discovered I could play the bugle (I had played trumpet in grade school), I became a "sergeant" and tootled during formations for visiting generals.

Miss Charlotte Haxall Noland, Foxcroft School, circa 1943

Demanding as she could be, Miss Charlotte also had a good sense of fun and was a fearless horsewoman, riding sidesaddle after smashing her right leg. She taught me how to ride sidesaddle and with Miss Greble, another teacher, we made an unbeatable hunt team!

Miss Charlotte loved to foxhunt and was joint master of the Middleburg Hunt for fourteen years, where she rode with General George S. Patton Jr. (then a major), who was stationed outside of Washington, D.C., in the 1930s. She often told the story of winning a $100 wager with Patton regarding who was the best rider. It seems that once when they were out hunting, the fox had slipped into an enclosed paddock surrounded by four-foot stone walls with riders on top. Patton pulled the field up to go through a gate, while Miss Charlotte galloped by, jumped in and out of the paddock, and kept going. Needless to say, she won the bet. When I met General Patton in Europe during the war, he acknowledged the story, commenting, "Charlotte was crazy, but won that $100 fair and square!"

Foxcroft had an exceptional faculty of well-educated, devoted teachers who sometimes despaired of their headmistress. On occasion, Miss Charlotte would come into evening study hall and announce that if anyone wanted to go on a ride, they should be at the stables in half an hour. (Having already been tipped off, I would have the horses saddled and waiting.) Of course, this cleared out study hall, much to the teachers' frustration.

It wasn't long before I landed in trouble. That October, I worked with the girls to set up a Halloween spook house. One of the challenges was to slide blindfolded down a rope from the second floor. The teachers all had a hissy fit about safety, but Miss Charlotte went through the entire spook house and emerged with a big grin: "At last we are having fun!" Later in the spring, the teachers all thought I should be fired when, after a long hot ride, I let the girls skinny-dip in Goose Creek. Miss Charlotte stood up for me, saying she only wished she could have been there too.

Soon after my arrival, Miss Charlotte insisted that I attend all the faculty meetings. She said I was the only one, other than herself, who would speak up for students whom the teachers wanted to expel for some minor infraction.

One of the best things about Miss Charlotte was she trusted my judgment. Soon after I arrived at Foxcroft, a black stable boy—in a fit of rage—killed a man who was messing with his wife. If he went to jail, his family would starve. The judge, recognizing that this had been a crime of passion, told him that if he could find someone to guarantee his behavior, he could continue to work. I took his request to Miss Charlotte, who told me that the decision was mine; since I was head of the Riding Department, he was my employee and I would have to be responsible for his actions. He stayed and never gave me any cause for regret.

It was at Foxcroft where I really learned how to teach kids to ride. At age twelve I had charged friends 25 cents an hour for lessons and I did some teaching at Chatham Hall, but at Foxcroft I was fully in charge. The biggest challenge was matching horses to riders' skill and experience. I wanted the girls to have fun, but safety was most important. I am proud to say that there were no accidents during the two years I ran the riding department.

The Middleburg Hounds hunted three times a week. I could take the better riders out on Saturday and was given permission to follow hounds on Tuesday and Thursday afternoons, if I could find the hunt. I would call the huntsman, who would tell me the general territory they would be riding across that day. The girls and I had a great time tracking the hunt and then following, by checking for signs left on the ground and listening to the horn and hounds.

Halfway through my first year, Miss Charlotte gave me a thoroughbred mare that no one else could ride. Playtoy turned out to be the best animal I ever owned. I won the Middleburg Point-to-Point on her and she hunted beautifully for me. In May 1944, just before I left Foxcroft, my friend Liz Whitney let me breed Playtoy to her outstanding stud Bon Nuit. That summer, however, the mare was killed by lightning in a field, so I never realized the prize I might have had.

Playtoy, winner Middleburg Point-to-Point, spring 1944

FIVE

General George S. Patton Jr.

I wanted to join the war effort and, with Miss Charlotte's support, began to take flying lessons at a nearby airfield in 1943. The Women's Ferry Command would accept me if I had some flying time. I soon realized, however, that my bum arm couldn't take the strain of pulling the Piper Cub out of free falls. Miss Charlotte, who was on the national board of the American Red Cross, subsequently helped me to join the ARC. At that time you were supposed to be at least twenty-five years old to be given a foreign assignment, and I was only twenty-three, but Miss Charlotte convinced them that if I was mature enough to run her entire riding department at Foxcroft, then I certainly was mature enough to go overseas with the Red Cross.

Off I went with the ARC the summer of 1944 for six weeks of training. I began in Washington, D.C., with several dozen girls who were all much older than I. Some were recently widowed (due to the war) and some were simply looking for husbands. Most were "good eggs" who were as excited as I was to go overseas. Inevitably, I found trouble. One afternoon, we were piling onto a bus to go to a class. It was packed and as I squeezed onto the bottom step, the girls behind me yelled that I should get off and take a later bus with them. The driver, however, couldn't see me and closed the door just as I turned to step down. The door closed on my neck (the rubber saved me), but I rode past three stops with my head sticking out before my friends convinced the driver to stop.

After a month's training and a brief stint at Langley Air Force Base, I was ready to graduate and go overseas. I was already engaged to Don McLean, whom I had met in Watertown when he attended a Princeton University ROTC program at Camp Drum. Don was furious that I wouldn't marry him before he shipped overseas, but I was determined to be part of the war effort and stayed single. He was even madder when I beat him out and arrived in Europe before he did!

Mary Spencer Kimball, American Red Cross, July 1944

As I prepared to go to Europe with the American Red Cross in July 1944, Mother and Daddy came down to Washington, D.C., to say their good-byes. My deployment orders were secret, but they knew I'd be shipping out soon. At one point, Mother turned to me and said, "Spencer, I don't think we'll ever see each other again." Now, Mother rarely cried or showed her emotions, so in some embarrassment I told her that she was being silly; I'd be home soon and, after all, she had to put on my wedding to Don. Her comment, however, was not entirely a surprise. She had told me earlier in the summer that she had been diagnosed with breast cancer, after spending several months in a body-cast following the fall that broke her back in 1939. She had not told Daddy, because he would have fretted unnecessarily and was extremely involved in his work on the New York State Supreme Court. But she felt someone in the family should know.

A few weeks later, I was sent to New York City and found myself standing on a dock looking up at the biggest ship I'd ever seen. It turned out we were sailing on the *Queen Mary*! Eight women were assigned to a room, two portholes up from the water. I took a top bunk, figuring that if people were seasick I'd at least stay dry.

Soon after departure and without explanation, the captain ordered us to return to our cabins below deck. Curiosity trumping prudence, I hid under a lifeboat on the top deck, where I watched Prime Minister Winston Churchill come on board with his entourage. We had a U.S. Navy escort halfway across the Atlantic, at which point the British Navy took charge. We zigzagged to avoid German submarines; huge guns were set up on the back of the ship. What an adventure!

There were 1500 troops on board, so most of us spent our days entertaining the soldiers. I kept my nose clean, but some of the women played around and spent more time below decks than above. I retained my naïveté throughout the war, but sure learned a lot about what makes the world go round.

By 1942, the American Red Cross had set up a number of service clubs throughout England and Scotland to offer hospitality to U.S. military personnel on leave or in hospital. The clubs, however, were inaccessible to many soldiers in remote places, so the new Red Cross commissioner (Harvey Gibson) determined there should be clubs on wheels, dubbed Clubmobiles. London Green Line buses were outfitted with a good-sized kitchen, including a built-in doughnut machine and a Primus stove to heat coffee prepared in fifty-cup urns. One side of the bus folded down to make a counter for serving the coffee and doughnuts, and there was a lounge in the back. Three American Red Cross girls were assigned to each Clubmobile with a local driver.

By the time I landed in London, August 1944, a small number of Clubmobiles were being sent to the continent to serve soldiers on the front lines. That was where the action was and all the girls competed for such an assignment. First, however, I had to learn how to drive a two-and-a-half-ton truck and to make coffee and doughnuts in massive quantities. After London, I was sent up to Scotland to help out at an American Air Force base where wounded boys, back from the battlefield, were waiting to be flown home to the States. Discouraged that the selection criteria for Clubmobilers being sent to Europe were age and experience, I feared I'd spend the war dodging buzz bombs in England. But I must have the luck of the Irish, because in November 1944 I was handed orders to head to France.

As much as I tried to mind my Ps and Qs, while crossing the English Channel I managed to get myself into serious trouble, which very nearly ended my Red Cross career. We were on a landing craft, tied alongside a Liberty ship, held up due to German mines in the area. Bored with the long wait, I happily accepted an invitation from the sailors to climb aboard and explore their ship. I had a great time until my ARC commanding officer caught wind of this little adventure and ordered me back to the landing craft. She told me I had gone AWOL and that when we reached Paris, I'd be court-martialed and sent home. I was desolate and, in tears, shared this news with some of my good friends. At Le Havre, we boarded a train to Paris that seemed too quickly to be taking me to disaster. But just before we arrived, one of my ARC buddies whispered that she had found the CO in the baggage car with an officer. She stuck up for me and the CO quietly dropped all her charges. What a relief!

Prestwick, Scotland, September 1944

In Paris, to repair my reputation as a good worker, I immediately signed up with a local ARC canteen, while most of the girls toured the sights and partied. Within two weeks I was recalled to join the Group L Clubmobile, stationed with General George Patton's Third Army in Germany. I arrived in early December 1944 and was assigned to the *Sioux Falls*—the Clubmobile captained by Jean Gordon, General Patton's niece.

General George S. Patton Jr. was the last of the great people who had an enormous influence on my life. I count him as my fifth mentor.

In Europe with the Third Army

Jean Gordon was in her thirties and immediately took me under her wing. A Boston blue blood, she was no snob—just a sincere hard worker with a quiet sense of humor. Jean had grown up in Paris and spoke beautiful Parisian French with her "Uncle Georgie," who had been stationed there some years with his wife, Beatrice Ayer. Her Parisian French, however, was of no use in the French countryside, when one afternoon we stopped at a farmhouse because I desperately needed to pee. The farmer just stared at her blankly when she tried to find me a *salle de bain.* But when I asked "Avez-vous une toilette pour l'enfant?" he burst out laughing and took me around the back of the house to a corncrib. With hogs snuffling nearby, the entire family watched as I did my business.

Not long after that I was invited to accompany Jean to dinner at Patton's headquarters. This man was a true gentleman! He never used "cuss words" in front of women and always stood up when a lady entered the room. Not all generals, however, were as disciplined as Patton. I will always remember a party he hosted for General Eisenhower. Ike got drunk, as did another Red Cross girl (a shrewd opportunist who stuck to Jean Gordon like a barnacle and managed to get in all the photos with visiting generals). I can see her now sitting on Ike's lap, cooing to him and patting his bald head. I was so disgusted that I refused to vote for Eisenhower when he later ran for president. I still thought men my father's age should be gentlemen.

The press ruined Patton's reputation at every chance it got. He refused to let reporters up on the front lines, because he distrusted their discretion and worried that they would write reports giving the Germans clues to our troop movements. The press had crucified him when he had slapped a shell-shocked soldier in Sicily. Patton had been going through wards of the wounded, giving out Purple Hearts. Badly shaken by what he had seen, when he asked a weeping boy who was not hurt what his problem was and the boy said "Scared!" Patton lost it.

With his pearl-handle pistols and spit-and-polish riding boots, General Patton could be quite intimidating. Underneath the gruffness, however, I found a kind and caring person. He knew how to lead troops and talked to them in their own (sometimes crude) language. Yes, he was strict, but I admired this as much as I admired my mother's strictness. His men knew he would never ask them to take risks he was unwilling to take himself. If there was a problem or death in one of his soldiers' families, he was the first to know about it and even under fire would try to tell the soldier himself.

Before taking up command of the Third Army, Patton bought an English bull terrier in England, which he named "Willie"—short for William the Conqueror.

> "No bastard ever won a war by dying for his country. He won it by making the other poor dumb bastard die for his country."
>
> —*George S. Patton Jr.*

Willie was cared for by Sergeant Meeks, a black soldier who had been Patton's aide during World War I. Meeks had retired, but when Patton knew he was going overseas again, he personally asked him to re-enlist. Sergeant Meeks was the only person who could tell the General when he was wrong. Meeks would talk to Willie about what their "Boss" was up to, whether the General should do this or that . . . and Patton listened!

When the Third Army moved into Germany, Willie had his own bronze bust of Hitler, which he "anointed" every morning. After the war, when Willie's boss and our ARC Clubmobile were quartered close together, Willie would take my dachshund puppy for walks. Very protective, Willie reminded me of White Rock, my childhood guardian.

The General, who was a foxhunting friend of Miss Charlotte's, seemed to like me, and I loved his cavalry stories about riding with General John J. Pershing on the 1916 Punitive Expedition against Pancho Villa in Mexico. Patton had a passion for horses and had thoroughly studied the history of their use in warfare. He honored the horse as a comrade who, if treated with kindness and given proper care, would never let you down.

I did, however, get into trouble with Patton twice. The first time was in Luxembourg, where a GI traded me a small German motorcycle for a few packs of cigarettes. I brought my new toy back in our Clubmobile, which was empty because we had taken the machines off the trucks and were making doughnuts in a large garage. Deciding to ride my "bike" from our living quarters back to the garage, about a mile down the road, I hadn't even taken off when Patton came stomping over. Didn't I know that gas was rationed?! Having scolded me sternly, he then said that he too had been given a motorcycle. He challenged me to a race, after which both cycles would become the property of the U.S. Army. Needless to say, he won.

The second rebuke I had from General Patton was near the end of the war, when we were serving outside a newly liberated German prisoner-of-war camp. While we were handing out doughnuts and coffee, a bunch of ex-prisoners drove up in a convertible Mercedes. The driver tossed the keys up to me saying, "We knocked out a German and took his car, but because we will be drinking tea in England in a few short hours, you can have it!" Delighted, I drove the Mercedes home that night, parking it in front of our ARC house. Some hours later I heard a loud voice downstairs yelling, "Whoever owns that car, come down here at once!" It was the General, who again chewed me out for wasting gas. He relented a little, however, and let me take the red leather seats to put in our jeep.

General George S. Patton Jr.

Mother closely followed my adventures during the war. She had been offered the job of U.S. liaison with the ARC in England, but there was no way she could leave Daddy, so she remained in Watertown as chairman of the Jefferson County chapter of the Red Cross. She wrote Patton about me and he wrote her back—a letter I found with all my war correspondence when I came home in 1945. Unfortunately, most of my war letters aren't worth rereading. Patton warned us repeatedly against leaking information to the enemy, so I never mentioned precisely where I was or with which army unit. My letters contain little more than messages from soldiers I'd met who lived near Watertown—to be passed on to their families—and requests for more toiletries from

Mr. Herrick's drugstore. I also have no photographs of myself with General Patton; he refused to pose with any woman, for fear the press would sensationalize the relationship back home.

Although my brother Craig and I were very different and sometimes at odds (he called me "Piano-legs Kimball," I called him "Mr. Goody Two-Shoes"), we were in touch constantly when I was in Europe. His asthma would have permitted him to sit out the war at home, but he was determined to go overseas and in order to pass the army physical, he lived in a motel for a month. He was sent to Africa first and later stationed in England, where he was badly hurt by German buzz bombs. The army wanted to send him home, but he slipped out of the hospital one night and tracked down his unit, which was now in Germany. His determination was remarkable, and he came home with a Silver Star.

Not long before the Germans surrendered, Patton was sent to liberate Buchenwald, one of the Nazis' biggest concentration camps. It essentially was a "photo-op" to publicize Nazi atrocities; reporters and photographers from around the world were there. Fearful that the enlisted men, after witnessing the horrors, might start killing off the SS guards, Patton decided to take the Red Cross in with him to "normalize" the situation. So Jean Gordon, Betty South and I spent several hours outside the gates handing out coffee and doughnuts.

You could smell that damned concentration camp from miles away. Germans lined the roads wailing that they hadn't known what was going on at the camp. I was so angered by their dishonest blindness that if I'd had a gun I might have used it. We saw piles of dead bodies, covered in lime, in open ditches. We saw the ovens where the Nazis had incinerated thousands of prisoners. We watched the barely alive crawl out of filthy sheds, only to die at our feet. It was sickening. Afterwards, General Patton gave each of us four Battle Stars to wear. He felt we deserved them for all we had seen and done.

In late May 1945, following the German surrender, I took a few days' leave to visit my fiancé, Don, who was briefly in hospital in Nancy, France. This little jaunt nearly ended with me being reported as AWOL!

I had hitched a ride to Nancy on an army truck but, at the hospital, I met several friendly pilots from the air base who were more than happy to give me a lift back to my outfit. Once in the air, however, I found myself "kidnapped" and taken to another base for several days. The boys were "gentlemen" and I came to no harm, but I learned about "war mischief" that was very upsetting. Laughing over drinks, they told stories about U.S. fighter pilots strafing German farmers and animals—anything that moved—just for the fun of it. It was hard to reconcile this behavior with the ideals of the U.S. war effort, but I wasn't so naïve as not to know that soldiers from any army could commit criminal acts.

Once, when I had been waiting at a crossroads for my Clubmobile, a truckload of GIs passed by, whistling and shouting at me. I was happy to wave at them, but when several climbed down from the truck and started towards me, I beat a hasty retreat up the hill to a convent school, full of nuns and children. At that moment I was much more scared of the GIs than of the Germans.

Clubmobilers with GIs, February 1945

Back with my Red Cross unit, we were still busy feeding and entertaining troops slowly being sent home. I spent a great summer sightseeing in the rolling German countryside, including a visit to Adolf Hitler's "crow's nest" in the Southern Alps, where some GIs and I "liberated" a couple of bottles of port from Hitler's private stock. We also stopped by Heinrich Himmler's beautiful chateau on Lake Tangeray and I picked up one of his oil paintings to take home as a memento. (Unfortunately, it was stolen out of my footlocker when we hit the States, along with a German Luger I'd bought for my Dad.) I went white-water rafting and rode with "Hap" Gay and General Patton on lovely horses given to him by the Russians, who had stolen them from the Germans. I only wish I could have ridden one of the Lippizan horses General Patton saved from destruction.

Despite what was written about him in the press, I didn't experience Patton as an arrogant egomaniac. The summer of 1945 I accompanied him and a group of officers on a boat trip around one of the mountain lakes. The officers were fawning over him, which he indeed loved, so when he pulled out his revolver and with one shot took out a duck, they all cheered, congratulating him on his marksmanship. Unfortunately, it was a diving duck, and sitting in the back of the boat, I saw it pop up again after we had cruised by. I tapped him on the sleeve and whispered what I had seen. He whispered back that I had seen NO SUCH THING, but I could see his mouth twitching with a smile as he turned to rejoin the officers' conversation.

Patton publicly declared that after mopping up Europe, he wanted to go to China and finish off the Japs. We all wanted to go with him! This of course came to nothing when in August the Americans dropped bombs on Hiroshima and Nagasaki, resulting in surrender and the end of the war. At this point, I told Don that I would marry him in Europe; General Patton had agreed to take me down the aisle in Daddy's absence. I felt badly that Mother would miss the wedding that she'd been preparing for all these years, but knew she would understand that I wanted to work longer with the Red Cross. ARC headquarters had given me permission to marry and be attached to Don's outfit, until he was sent home the spring of 1946.

When my Clubmobile came home one evening in early September, after a week in the mountains with an ack-ack (anti-artillery) outfit, General Patton was waiting for me at our house with his aide, Major Pat Merle-Smith. Patton beckoned me into the library, where he informed me—as best he could—that my mother had been killed in a car accident in Watertown.

Driving a Red Cross station wagon, Mother was headed to a child care center she had set up with federal funds to allow women to work during the war. On the way she had stopped off to tell her former Italian housekeeper, Florence, that arrangements had been made for the body of Florence's only son—killed overseas—to be brought home for burial. This was a boy Mother had encouraged to graduate from high school and join the U.S. Coast Guard. He had become one of the youngest captains ever, when a drunken sailor shot him in a brawl. After a short visit, Mother headed across town and, I guess, just wasn't paying attention. She misjudged the speed of a tractor-trailer full of oil, which slammed into her right front fender when she pulled out across Bellew Avenue.

Carola Kimball, chairman American Red Cross, Jefferson County, 1943

A SOLDIER'S BURIAL

Not midst the chanting of the Requiem Hymn,
Nor with the solemn ritual of prayer,
Neath misty shadows from the oriel glass,
And dreamy perfume of the incensed air
Was he interred
But the subtle stillness after fight,
And the half light between the night and the day,
We dragged his body all besmeared with mud,
And dropped it, clod-like, back into the clay.
Yet who shall say that he was not content,
Or missed the prayers, or drone of chanting choir,
He who had heard all day the Battle Hymn
Sung on all sides by a thousand throats of fire.
What painted glass can lovelier shadows cast
Than those the evening skies shall ever shed,
While, mingled with their lilt, Red Battle's Sun
Completes in magic colors o'er our dead
The flag for which they died.

—*George S. Patton Jr.*

The station wagon spun around and she was thrown twenty-nine feet onto the pavement. She never knew what hit her and died instantly.

General Patton told me that I must go home to be with my father. I said, "No, sir, I want to stay with my friends." He said, "That's fine, but I'll have a plane take you to Paris tomorrow at 6:00 a.m." I protested, but was on the plane the following morning and from Paris flew on to the States and Watertown two days later.

Home from the War

I thought my world had ended. Daddy was a disaster when I got home and began to drink heavily. I tried my best to keep the house running like Mother would have, but it didn't work. Daddy's behavior upset me so much that I called Washington asking to re-enlist with the Red Cross. I was accepted but, when Daddy heard about my plans, he cried and promised to stop drinking and fooling around with women. Fortunately, Alf was there to put him to bed when the Judge staggered home from the pubs. My brother Craig returned from Europe and married Grace O'Dare at the Mill in Sackets Harbor. I was so unravelled that I wrote Don to break off our engagement. Life just didn't make any sense any more and I didn't know what was going to happen next.

In December 1945 came news of General Patton's death in a car accident. I cried and cried. It seemed so unfair after his brilliance during the war. He had been planning to retire to Middleburg, Virginia, and had invited his niece Jean Gordon to join the family there. Patton's death devastated Jean, especially because she was having so much trouble with her family in Boston. Soon after she returned home in the fall, a GI she'd met in Europe had shown up at her front door, parking his delivery truck on the street. Her mother not only refused to let him see Jean, but also raked him up and down for daring to come to the front door. The likes of him belonged at the back, with the servants. Jean called me in tears that her mother was still trying to control her life.

Pam Schweppe, a wonderful Clubmobiler I'd worked with in Europe, invited all of us who had served with General Patton down to her parents' place in Scarsdale, New York, for a reunion in mid-January 1946. Delighted to be able to escape all the confusion at home, I wrote Jean saying how much I looked forward to seeing her at "Schweppe's," giving her the time and address. The party began at 7:30 p.m. We knew Jean was staying in New York City at a friend's apartment, so we didn't immediately worry that she was late; she had probably missed the early train. An hour and a half later, police were at the door asking for a "Mary Kimball." Jean had stuck her head in the oven and killed herself. The police had found my letter to Jean on the kitchen table.

Jean's suicide so upset me that I wrote her mother a blistering letter accusing her of driving Jean to despair. A vicious letter, it is one of the few things I have done in my life of which I am ashamed.

Dogs, Cats, Horses, Ponies, Goats, Rabbits and Children

SIX

Marriage, Boston and Syracuse, New York, 1946–1957

By the time Don arrived home from Europe, I had reconsidered and decided to go ahead with the wedding in August. With Mother gone, Aunt Jessie stepped in and made sure the silver, champagne and my wedding dress were all in order. Dr. Lee came up from Chatham Hall to officiate and the reception was at the Mill, where Alf had outdone himself with the garden. We cut the cake with a German sword Don had brought back from the war.

Marriage, Donald Addison McLean, July 28, 1946 Watertown, New York

Don came from a large McLean "clan" in Binghamton, New York. His dad was president of McLean's Department Store—the family business—but Floyd had been a cavalry officer in World War I and preferred the out-of-doors to a desk job. In contrast, Don's mother, Lucille, belonged to every social club and women's auxiliary in town. The first time I visited Don in Binghamton, I met his Grandmother McLean, who to Lucille's horror, promptly took me into the living room to show me the jar containing her recently removed gallstones!

I liked Floyd, and when he and Lucille had come up to meet my parents before the war, Daddy and I had taken him fishing while Lucille played bridge with Mother's friends. Floyd considered himself a near-professional fisherman and had brought with him a box full of fancy lures. Daddy and I used the night crawlers I always dug for bait. Within an hour, I had caught several fish while Floyd had none. I could see he was becoming upset, so I offered to switch sides of the boat. But I continued to catch fish, while he went home almost empty-handed. Fortunately, he didn't hold it against me and told Don that he would be disinherited if he let me get away. Tragically, Floyd died of a heart attack while taking his mother to church, just before Don returned from Europe.

Boston

After the wedding and a honeymoon trip to Canada, Don and I moved to Boston, where he began an MBA at the Harvard Business School. To be honest, this wasn't the happiest time of my life. Mother had just died, Don spent all day in classes, and I ended up with a job in a print shop. It was hot, dirty work and when I came home there was Don waiting for dinner, after which he'd go out for drinks with his classmates. I quickly became pregnant, which made the job even more difficult. The baby was due in the spring of 1947 and all seemed well until the eighth month, when I could no longer feel any movement. I went to the doctor, who told me the baby had died but because Boston was such a Catholic town, he wouldn't do an abortion. I flew home to Watertown, where my childhood doctor immediately put me in the hospital and removed the baby.

The next year was better. Recovered, I promptly became pregnant again and "Hoot"—Donald Addison McLean Jr.—was born Easter Sunday 1948, in Watertown. Don was awarded his MBA and we moved to Syracuse, New York, where Don had accepted a job with Dey Brothers Department Store. We rented briefly, bought our first house on Homewood Drive in Syracuse, and then moved to 4ll Elm Street in Fayetteville, just south of the city. Our home was almost equidistant from both Watertown and Binghamton, so it was an easy drive to visit our families.

Eight months gone—February 1948

Syracuse and Fayetteville

After the war, I had no animals for three to four years. Once we were settled in Syracuse, however, dogs, cats, ponies, horses, goats and rabbits soon found their way to our house. Our first dog was Mark Down, a boxer given to us by friends. Mark Down was really Don's pet, although he liked to play games with Hoot and I taught him to pull a sled. He just wasn't that enthusiastic about kids and, sadly, was hit by a car a few years later. Unfortunately, cars also hit Vitamin the cat and our next dog, Checkers, a miniature schnauzer. Since there were no leash laws, the animals ran freely on city streets.

Cynthia Kimball McLean was born November 1950, when we still lived on Homewood Drive. Mary Wolcott McLean was born July 1952, after we moved to the larger house in Fayetteville. Don adored the children, but was none too pleased with my propensity to wait until the last minute to head to the hospital. Because I'd spent so many months in and out of hospitals as a child, where doctors tried to repair my smashed arm, I gagged at the mere thought of ether. Consequently, Cindy was born on a gurney en route to the delivery room and "Woo" was born prematurely on the front seat of Don's brand-new car! Once Woo was safely installed in an incubator, Don raced home to scrub down his new seat covers, which just were never the same.

In short order, more animals showed up. I had no horses at the time, but soon after Woo's birth, my old friend Jane Dunn gave me Topper. Jane and I knew each other from horse shows in the 1930s, when I was competing in jumping events on Robin.

Topper was a lovely old paint pony that Jane was going to put down if I didn't take him. Easily persuaded, I renovated a large dog kennel on our half-acre property into a small stable. I talked to the neighbors, who didn't seem to mind my having a pony in the backyard, and early one morning Topper was delivered. The pony whinnied and whinnied; having come from a large stable, he was lonesome. So when the milkman arrived, I asked him where I could find a goat to keep Topper company. That afternoon, after his milk deliveries, he brought over a huge white goat named Ichabod.

When Don came home that night I told him that the pony had arrived. He was so excited that he insisted on going out immediately to see him. I tried to stall him, figuring I'd break the news about Ichabod after dinner. It was dark and cold, but Don was not to be stopped. Out he went through a foot of snow, but was back in no time looking very perplexed. "What's going on out there?" he demanded. "I didn't find the pony, but something went *Baaaah* at me when I opened the barn door!"

Ichabod was a character and at times could be a terror. One of our neighbors was terrified of animals and had the misfortune to be outdoors one afternoon when Ichabod escaped his pen. He chased her home, went right through the screen door on the back porch and followed her up the front stairs. Hearing her screams, I came running and found my neighbor atop a high chest, with Ichabod dancing around at her feet bleating loudly!

Another time, Ichabod managed to slip in the back door during a party and goosed a guest searching for olives on the bottom shelf of the icebox. (Don nearly got slapped for that one!) Ichabod then dashed into the living room, jumping on the furniture and dropping little black "jelly beans" all over the carpet. He also managed to eat most of a pack of cigarettes, spitting out the filters, before we were able to drag him out. Don threatened to turn Ichabod into goat stew.

A more sensible animal, Topper gave Hoot, Woo and Cindy their first riding lessons. He became a great driving pony with an old sleigh I fixed up in the basement, and happily pulled the kids and their friends around Fayetteville on a long bobsled.

Snowy day with TenEyck children

Ichabod joined us on many of these snowy rides. I'd hook Topper to the bobsled and then tie a kid's sled onto a harness I'd made for the goat. Topper would set off at a good clip with Ichabod right behind. One day an old man passed this strange procession and nearly drove his car into a telegraph pole because he was laughing so hard.

Topper also helped out in the fall when we were raking up leaves. One fall afternoon, I tied him to the leaf sweeper and, with Cindy and Woo on his back, led him around the lawn collecting the leaves. When it was full, I would drag it down to the street and empty the leaves into a fire that Hoot was tending. Eventually the girls went off to play, Hoot was busy putting out flying sparks and I simply wasn't paying attention. Topper walked through the fire and, while he stood clear on the other side, the leaf sweeper caught fire behind him! I ran Topper all over the damp lawn, thinking this would put out the fire, but I was wrong and the leaf sweeper burned to a crisp.

With three children, I thought I'd never *really* ride again. But one day driving down a country road in Manlius, I spotted this "thing" lying by a fence. I stopped and found a half-dead yearling covered with flies—just a bag of bones. Very upset, I drove up to the farmhouse and asked about him. It seems the colt had been brought in from the West and en route had developed shipping fever. The farmer was just waiting for it to die so he could bury it in his manure pile. I said, "Okay, let me have him." The farmer was delighted, so I went home and called Jane Dunn, who had a pickup. We loaded this pathetic little thing into her truck and I took him home.

Two doors down the street lived a retired veterinarian, who took care of all the small rabbits and creatures Hoot brought him. When I called, he came right over but took one look and said, "Spencer, I'm sorry, but this animal isn't going to make it and if by some miracle it does live, it won't be any good." Refusing to give up, I spent months nursing him back to health. Once on his feet, I taught him first to drive and then to carry a rider. He became a real "pet"; the only problem was that he learned quickly how to open gates and barn doors. Alf came down from Watertown for a visit and christened him "Slipstring"—a British term for a convict on the lam. Well named, Slip spent the next twenty years escaping pastures and "slipping strings" when I wasn't looking.

Once I had Slip, I had to find a horse for Don. He never was a great rider, but had spent several summers on a dude ranch in Montana and was familiar with horses. Some months later, a woman I hardly knew gave me a small bay horse she had bought off a neighbor who was badly mistreating him. We called him Smokey, and he turned out to be a quiet quarter horse with a nice temperament. Don had fun with him; Smokey's only fault was that he cribbed.

Even before Smokey arrived, I had moved Slip over to Chessie TenEyck's barn around the corner. Not only was there not enough room for the horses in the converted dog kennels, but the kid next door also had started to take potshots at the horses with his BB gun. Chessie's place was closer to riding trails too. Don and I rode most weekends, with Hoot trailing behind on Topper. During the week I often rode with Helen Bodie, even in the dead of winter when we had to use six-inch cigarette holders to smoke with our heavy gloves on.

Accustomed as I was to taking care of horses, motherhood was an entirely new experience for me. I came home from riding one day and found Don working in his study, but Cindy (age three) had disappeared. Slightly panicked, I noticed that the front door was ajar and then spotted little footprints in the snow. I followed them across the street, up the hill, past the firehouse and into the drugstore, where I found a barefoot Cindy at the candy counter with a very disapproving clerk. Another time Helen and I had been out on the horses for a good hour before I remembered I had forgotten to pick up the babysitter. Thank goodness for a small town where people didn't immediately call the police over child neglect!

Horses certainly did not occupy all my time. I joined the Junior League and continued to do volunteer work with the Red Cross. The Elm Street house had once been surrounded by formal gardens, so I also joined the garden club, thinking I might be able to do what Alf had done at the Mill. I cleaned up the garden and then proudly invited the garden club for lunch and advice. The president took one look and gasped: The old bulbs and plantings had rotted or gone to seed, which made them poisonous for children and animals! That was the end of the garden. I ploughed it under and stuck with flower arranging, which won me a blue ribbon at the next show.

Hoot was born cross-eyed and required remedial surgery. I took him to a specialist in Watertown, which also allowed me to see Daddy and his new wife, Ruby. I could take a train from Syracuse and in two hours be at the downtown Watertown train station, right next to the Hotel Woodruff, where Daddy and Ruby lived during the winter. In the summer Don and I would drive the kids up to see them at the Mill in Sackets Harbor, which was eerily quiet after the army closed Madison Barracks in 1945.

A new mother and wife, I dressed up and even wore perfume when I took Hoot to the doctor's office for consultations. I wanted to impress everyone with my new-found maturity. One morning, however, I had to leave Hoot—eyes bandaged—in the waiting room while I used the lavatory down the hall. Asked by a concerned nurse where his mother was and what she looked like, Hoot calmly said, "You can't miss her. She's short, she wears a long camel-hair coat and she smells like horses!" I guess I just wasn't cut out to be a sophisticate.

STIRRUP CUP FARM, MANLIUS

Once Don was convinced that horses would be our "family sport," we needed to find a place with more acreage and a larger barn. The summer of 1956 we moved to Manlius, a more rural area near Fayetteville, where we bought an old dairy farm with one hundred acres of land. Besides the barn, still full of rusting milking equipment, there was a big chicken coop, a stone house for candling eggs, and a small farmhouse with a big root and preserves cellar. We were truly in the country, where telephone service was still a party line and I had to learn to cook on a huge cast-iron stove.

Stirrup Cup Farm, 1956

To cut our taxes, we became Stirrup Cup Farm, and Don decided to save even more money by leasing out the fields to a farmer, who would turn over half the hay crop to us at harvest time. The scheme wasn't a brilliant success. Don figured that after expenses and his labor hauling the hay bales to the barn (during which he badly sprained his ankle), he had saved about $17.32.

The winter before we moved to the farm, our last Syracuse dog arrived. I had been out at the dump when I heard a puppy crying somewhere in all the trash. I followed the yelps and off to the side found a cardboard box with three tiny puppies. The mother had been shot and two of the puppies were already dead, the third shaking violently from the cold. I took him home and he became Bullet, one of the best dogs we ever had. Bullet loved the farm, where he could roam through the fields and woods, but he didn't understand cars. I tried to lock him in the house when we went riding, but one day he escaped and was hit by a car when he ran across the road to catch up with the horses. Bullet was the first pet that the kids really loved and we had a big family cry. Briefly, we did have another mutt from the pound, but Sandy was big, did not know his own strength and jumped on the kids when they were sledding in the snow. We returned him to the pound.

Before we moved to Manlius, I put down an ailing Topper and returned Ichabod to his former owner. My good friend the horseshoer then gave me a pony for the kids—a little buckskin we called Stirrup First. Since the pony was unbroken, I decided to start her off with driving, which very nearly ended in disaster. It must have been February, a very cold winter day with a couple of feet of snow on the ground, when I hitched Stirrup up to our cutter and was driving her in circles around the pasture. Four-year-old Woo was sitting in a box in the back. Don was standing on top of the manure pile, filming us with his new movie camera, when suddenly Stirrup bolted. I couldn't stop her and turned the cutter towards the manure pile, where I nearly mowed Don down. I bailed out; the cutter flipped over and was dragged by the pony for a good twenty to thirty yards. Terrified, I ran over to untangle Woo, who looked up at me with a big smile and said, "Oooh, that was fun, let's do it again!"

Manlius turned out to be only a nine-month sojourn when Don accepted a new job with Stewart Dry Goods in Louisville, Kentucky. We left the spring of 1957 and I gave Stirrup to Fran Lane, our milkman, who in return hauled Slip and Smokey down to Kentucky for us.

SEVEN

Anchorage, Kentucky, 1957–1961

Before we moved the kids and animals to Kentucky, Don and I spent a few days in Louisville meeting his new colleagues and getting the lay of the land. A woman we met at a dinner party decided to make us her "project" and find us a place to live. She listened intently to our horse and people stories, then suddenly exclaimed, "You folks are different from most anyone else I know. You belong in Anchorage!"

She was right and we settled in Anchorage, a small village founded by a retired sea captain and a prosperous railwayman just north of Louisville. After renting for a few months, we found a house that came with several acres of trees and brush, just down the street from a still-lived-in 1782 log cabin built by the first settlers. I hired some hillbillies, hard workers, who cleared out a pasture for us, put up fences and built a foundation for a small two-stall barn we moved from a friend's backyard. Unfortunately, I'd forgotten to tell the hillbillies when the barn was coming and they protectively stopped the movers with a shotgun! Old Charlie Polk, the town marshal, had to be called in to sort out the standoff. A few weeks later, Slip and Smokey took up residence, the first of our many Kentucky horses and ponies.

Shortly after we arrived in Anchorage, we attended the annual St. Luke's Horse Show. One of the kids won a raffle, which resulted in us taking home a tiny golden puppy. He was supposedly a purebred cocker spaniel, but the pup's legs grew and grew; we suspected his daddy was a golden retriever. The kids named him Tucky, short for Kentucky. Not that smart but wonderful with children, Tucky was with us for the next fifteen years.

We did bring a cat down from New York, but when it attacked poor little Tucky, I spanked it and tossed it outdoors. I didn't see her again until a year later when I was visiting my good friend Nola Wolpert. There, sitting on Nola's back stoop, was that cat! Nola said it was a stray that had wandered in some months before. I kept my mouth shut and smiled. We had many cats in Anchorage, including a bobtailed Manx that produced several litters of kittens, to the delight of the kids.

Once the barn was up and the pasture enclosed, I bought a large paint pony from a farmer and named him Cochise. He turned out to be a bit too wild for the kids, so a year later I swapped him for Moreland Mousie, a good-looking bay mare about 14'1" hands. She arrived in the spring and to my surprise grew fatter and fatter over the summer. Suddenly in October, she foaled, producing a filly I named Misfit . . . by Mistake (Sire), out of Season (Dam).

When Smokey died of colic, I paid $400 for an American saddle horse for Don, the most money I ever paid for a horse. A two-year-old, already broken to saddle, he came from a well-known breeding farm, where he had been registered as "Plainview's Moon Glow." The only problem was that we rode primarily with people on thoroughbreds, who didn't like the saddle horse crowd or their "shaky tail" animals. Actually, this horse looked like a thoroughbred except for his "pin ears" and somewhat Roman nose. In any case, I took him home, pulled his mane and changed his name to Warlock. The breeders hadn't yet cut his tail, so when I rode with friends who asked about his breeding, I told a fib and said I'd bought him from a farmer. Some years later, after Don won a point-to-point on him in Lexington, I confessed to his origins.

Spencer and Don, 1958

Warlock came along well but was a bit on the "nervy" side, and Don was still something of a novice around horses. One morning when we were running late to hunt with the Oldham County Hounds, Don tied Warlock's head tightly at the front of our new horse trailer, then jumped in the car and took off. He was driving around corners much too fast and I could hear thrashing going on in the trailer behind us. By the time we reached the hunt, Warlock was tangled up in his halter, had fallen in the trailer and was choking. I yelled at Don, but all we had was a small penknife off his key ring. I hacked and I sawed, finally releasing

Warlock before he collapsed. I was furious with Don, because I had told him to leave the horse with a loose tie, so that he had foot-room to brace himself when the car turned corners. To make my point, I drove Don home with his hands tied behind his back and blindfolded in the front of the trailer. I didn't speed, but he crashed around, couldn't keep his balance and later admitted that *maybe* I was right.

I also made Don ride Warlock without spurs or whip, especially out hunting. Years later, in Bedford, Cindy took Warlock to a Pony Club lesson with a well-known trainer who believed in "shaking up" a horse before jumping. Handing her a bat, he told her to whack Warlock several times behind the saddle just before the fence. She did, Warlock lunged, and off came Cindy on the far side, breaking her elbow in the process. Forget the whips.

Blue Grass Pony Club

Before we left Fayetteville, I had taken the training to start a horse chapter of the 4-H Club. In Kentucky, however, the 4-H was already working with the saddle horse people, so I backed off and began teaching kids in Anchorage how to ride. Then I met Dinwiddie Lampton, who not only had a pack of hounds he hunted on his farm in Oldham County, but also had established the Blue Grass Pony Club, following the lead of Mrs. Dean Bedford, who had brought Pony Club over from England in 1954. He had even brought in Miss Margaret Lindsley Warden—of USPC "white glove" fame—from Tennessee to help him start up a Pony Club properly.

In 1958, with a British friend who had ridden all her life, I set up a branch chapter of the Blue Grass Pony Club in Anchorage. Offering membership for $5 a year, plus free instruction, we ended up with several dozen boys and girls, some of whom had 4-H experience. A few of the kids were from wealthy families; others were the children of farmers and shopkeepers. Any child who could keep a pony in their backyard, or had access to one, was welcome. One day a little boy called and asked, "Mrs. McLean, I saved my money from delivering newspapers and bought a mule from the farmer next door. Can I join your pony club?" I said, "Sure!" He named his mule Beautiful and Beautiful became the cleanest, best cared for animal in the entire club.

Pony Club met at my house Saturday mornings. Using my own horses, I taught the kids how to muck out a stall and how to keep their animals happy with proper feed and grooming. They did all the work, including carrying buckets of hot water to melt the ice on my watering trough in the winter. The veterinarian wormed my horses as a demonstration for the kids; when I went out the next day to pitch manure, I found all kinds of worms in the poop, some still moving! So I bottled them in alcohol, and the next time the mothers didn't want to pay to worm their kids' horses, I brought out the bottle of worms. I never had any problem with worming again.

The Pony Clubbers were always enthusiastic and never missed a meeting. We played all kinds of games that everyone could do—some on horseback, some on foot. We went on trail rides and moonlight rides and camped overnight, tying the horses to trees. The kids rode in Nola and George Wolpert's annual horse show, winning ribbons in classes from Walk-Trot to Junior Hunter.

One of my favorite games was the scavenger hunt. Anchorage was small enough that the children could safely ride their ponies and horses all over town. I'd send out three kids as a team—one older and two younger so, if there was a problem, one could stay with the hurt child and the other go for help. One day, on the list of things they had to bring back to win the prize was a late-summer bird's nest; hair from a certain horse; a signature from a friend; and—to make it really hard—a set of false teeth. (The drugstore sold candy teeth for ten cents and I told the owner, if the kids came in, to give them the teeth and I'd pay him back later.) Noon was the deadline for returning with all ten of the "treasures" on the list. One team came in right on time, everyone grinning broadly that they had found everything. I was checking their collection when a little boy leaned over and whispered, "Mrs. McLean, can you hurry please? Those are my grandma's false teeth and I have to get them back to her so she can eat lunch!"

The local horse people—professional trainers, veterinarians, horseshoers, polo players and guys from the racetrack—were wonderful in sharing their time and expertise with the Pony Clubbers. The summer of 1959 the Louisville Polo Club invited both the boys and girls to use their practice field and swinging pen. So we started them on broomstick polo, with the kids using brooms and a volleyball. The ponies and horses took to it and we never had an accident. Once the kids felt comfortable swinging a broom on their horses, we challenged the men of Louisville's premier polo team to a match: They had to play left-handed and bareback. As I recall, the kids whomped them. I was really pleased that some of the boys continued to play polo right through college.

The following summer, I drove up to Vermont with June Faulkner and Ruby Rodes for Pony Club's first official instructors' clinic. We spent several weeks at Camp Teela

Wooket Camp with Alice Reidy, Sue Powers, Jack Fritz and Colonel Jack Burton. The instructors complained that my hands were not even over the horse's withers; or if my hands were even, that my elbows stuck out at odd angles. Finally I called them together, showed them that my right arm was about three inches shorter than my left (due to my childhood accident) and requested that they *please* decide whether they wanted my hands *or* my elbows even, because I couldn't do both. When we returned from Teela Wooket, Ruby, June and I began to plan our first Blue Grass Pony Club Rally at the fairgrounds.

Prior to the rally, my job was to lay out a cross-country course. A state penitentiary and several private farms bordered the fairgrounds. The landowners gave me permission to cut across their land, so one afternoon I went out by myself to mark the course with little strips of ribbon. I also found fallen trees that the kids could jump and gates they would have to open and close. Feeling quite pleased with the course, I headed back to my car, taking a path alongside the prison walls, where I waved at the armed guards above. Thinking it was a shortcut, I then started down a small path leading to a swamp with six-foot cattails. Suddenly I heard a sharp whistle and, turning, saw two guards racing towards me. It seems there had been a jailbreak that morning; they'd shot one prisoner but the others were still at large. The escapees, who were captured a few hours later, had made the trail I was following! I survived to tell the tale and the rally was a great success.

Involved with horses and Pony Club as I became, I still had a husband and three children—ages six, eight and ten—to tend. Happily, the kids all quickly made friends and became involved in local school and scouting activities, in addition to Pony Club. Cindy and Woo joined the Owl Creek Country Club swim team, Hoot was busy building things, and all three were able to ride their bikes all over town. During summer vacations, Don and I took them to explore the state: the Mammoth Caves in south-central Kentucky, the Old Kentucky Home in Bardstown and the log cabin where Abraham Lincoln was born. Generally they were good kids, but there were times when their squabbling drove me to distraction and I would look up to the heavens pleading, "Mother, *what do I do now?*" One afternoon, completely fed up, I told the kids I was calling the Anchorage Children's Home to see if they would take three naughty children off my hands. Huddled by the doorway to the kitchen, they listened to me "supposedly" making inquiries on the telephone. It turned out that the orphanage didn't have room and they were "saved." This kept them quiet for a few days.

Anchorage was still racially segregated when we lived there. The public school was entirely white; black children lived in Berrytown and Griffietown, which had their own schools. I hired an older couple from Berrytown, who helped out with the horses and babysat the kids. They seemed quite content with the status quo and were somewhat suspicious of civil rights workers coming down from the North preaching integration. I will always remember Fennelli's gas station on the edge of town. Fennelli served both black and white patrons, but they entered the building through different doors. The business was actually a single large room, with a wall running down the middle, and the owner served everyone from one long counter at the back. Although they couldn't occupy the same space, the men—black and white—often stood at the counter, chatting with each other around the dividing wall. It seemed an easy mix at the time, but of course within a few years race relations had entirely changed in the South.

It's amazing how the threads of one's earlier life reappear to be woven into the present. In Anchorage, Don and I became good friends with Dr. Glen Spurling, a neurosurgeon, who in December 1945 had been dispatched across the Atlantic to help General Patton following his car accident in Germany. He told me Patton would never have been able to climb back on a horse if he'd lived; he'd have been a miserable cripple. Knowing that Patton couldn't have tolerated living as a vegetable, I felt a little better about his untimely death.

Our Kentucky friends really knew how to have fun. When Alaska became a state in 1959, there was a big party at the Owl Creek Country Club. It was a costume party, so I borrowed a small burro, and Don and I went dressed as gold miners. I took the burro right into the club, where he spent the entire evening being fed snacks in the bar. I think they also gave him drinks, because he had to be carried out at the end of the night. Fortunately, he was fine the next morning.

The major event of the year, of course, was the Kentucky Derby at Churchill Downs. The "run for the roses" was always held the first weekend in May, with lavish parties and much drinking of mint juleps. One of the most prominent galas in Anchorage was a massive barbeque put on every year by the Honorable Order of Kentucky Colonels. Held the day after the derby, it was a very posh, by-invitation-only affair. In response, some of our good friends hosted an annual "Corporals" party next door, which was less prestigious but—since everyone came in costume—much more fun.

St. Luke's Horse Show, 1958

Horses did not consume all my time. Briefly I was a Girl Scout leader and I continued to work with the Junior League, collecting blood for the Red Cross from prisoners at the state penitentiary. For several years I also had roles in Mavis Magee's community theater productions—"Mummers and Minstrels." The shows were primarily comedies, and I starred in *A Most Unspotted Lily* about a real estate agent showing a couple the ins and outs of living in Anchorage. Half the town was in that play, including Don, who made a grand entrance down the center aisle on a bicycle. I do love the greasepaint and roar of the crowd; I think I'll come back as an actor in my next life.

Horse Country

Kentucky really is a horse lover's paradise. In addition to the annual derby, we took the kids to the Keeneland Race Track in Lexington, where they collected bags of discarded tickets, a few of which won them some money. We went to steeplechases, polo matches and yearling sales; we hunted with the Oldham County Hounds and participated in point-to-points. In Anchorage, we became increasingly involved in the St. Luke's Horse Show as gate judges and announcers; the kids won their first ribbons in St. Luke's walk-trot classes. The annual cleanup of the riding trails involved half the town, with the other half joining us for a huge barbeque after. In the winter we took the kids out to skate at Jack and Jean Gordon's farm, where we also met for beagling in the fall.

My favorite horse event was the annual Kentucky State Foxhunters Association Trials, which brought in packs of hounds from around the state to compete in conformation and working the land. It ran for an entire week and, in addition to the parties, involved riders following different packs of hounds in pursuit of a fox. Don stayed with the foxhunting people, but I joined up with some of the "night hunters"—good old boys who at home regularly took their hounds out at night to hunt gray foxes that could climb trees. Making camp, they'd sit for hours drinking whiskey from a local distillery and tell tall tales while their hounds worked. They could tell instantly, by "voice," which of their hounds had cornered or caught a fox. During the trials the night hunters rode in daylight; I always joined them because I knew the ride would be more fun and their hounds more likely to catch a fox.

One fall, I drove down with my old friend Colonel C.J. Cronin, who also planned to ride with the night hunters. Along the way, we came upon a dead fox on the side of the road. C.J. pulled over; I jumped out and cut off the fox's brush (tail), which I hid in the car until we were ready to ride. Stuffing the brush down my pants, I joined the night hunters and we were off. After several hours out with the hounds, we returned to the trailers, where the hunting people were already having tailgate parties. With no one except C.J. any the wiser, I pulled that brush out of my pants and came whooping in, shouting that we'd caught a fox and won the day! Several women exclaimed that they had seen that fox and weren't we lucky.

C.J. and I were having a good laugh behind the trailers when one of the older night hunters came over and demanded a look at this brush. He knew from the brush's dryness that it was not a fresh kill and scowled at me, before bursting into laughter and walking off without a word. Terribly pleased with myself, I went home happy until bedtime, when I began to itch terribly in my nether regions. The fox had had mange, which jumped to me when I stuffed its tail down my pants. At that point I had to tell Don what I'd done. With no sympathy, he just muttered, "Serves you right!" I itched for a week.

In the spring of 1959, I was pregnant with Caroline Craig McLean when Don was asked to be an outrider at a point-to-point at the Lamptons'. He was so excited to be asked, and I had him ride Slipstring because I knew Slip would be sensible around all the racing animals. Unable to ride myself, I stayed at the start of the course, but I could see Don stationed by a stone wall on a hill half a mile away. A few hours later, a horse fell over that fence, and while the rider jumped up immediately, the horse just lay

Kentucky State Foxhunter Association Trials, circa 1960

there. I watched Don carefully ride over to check out the situation, when suddenly Slip lay right down beside the horse with Don still holding on tight! Everyone laughed about this for the rest of the day, although Don didn't think it was so funny and never got on Slip again. (For the record, the horse was okay.)

Later that spring, still pregnant, I nearly met disaster at a horse show. Stationed at the gate, I saw a pony suddenly bolt across the ring and head right for me. Before I could get up from my seat, the pony sideswiped me, flipping me over backwards. I was terrified for the baby, but it turned out that she would have been a breech birth if not for the accident, which flipped her right-side up! "Craigie" was born two weeks later.

In 1961, Don was offered the job of vice president and treasurer of Lord & Taylor Department Store in New York City. I didn't want to move and our horse friends were furious with us for leaving, after they had so warmly included us in all their activities. But this was Don's opportunity to shine in the business world, so I buttoned my lip and began to pack. Following many wonderful but tearful bon voyage parties, we left for New York that summer. Today, after more than forty years, I still feel close to all the friends I made in Kentucky.

EIGHT

Bedford Village, New York, 1961–1974

After exploring several towns in New York and Connecticut, we landed in Bedford Village, a Westchester County community about fifty miles north of New York City. Still considered "horse country," Bedford had miles and miles of well-kept trails that ensured good riding through the woods, up and down hills, over streams and across great galloping meadows. We rented a house for a few months on the Hook Road, still dirt, and then bought a small farmhouse farther down the Hook from my old Chatham Hall classmate, Margot Woodle Marsh. Tucked into the woods at the end of a long driveway, the house came with eleven acres, a three-stall barn and three fenced pastures as well as a longhaired, six-toed black cat named Muffy, chickens, and a handful of fighting cocks. I sorted out schools for Hoot, Cindy and Woo; our only excitement in the first few months was the arrival of a hook and ladder from the fire department when two-year-old Craigie locked herself in the upper bathroom of our rented house.

Tucky-dog and the Manx cat had accompanied us on the drive from Kentucky; by late fall, Slipstring, Warlock and Moreland Mousie had moved into the barn. Mousie turned out to be too strong for the kids, so I sold her and set about collecting animals they could ride.

The summer of 1962, Don was busy with an architect building an addition to the house, while I added more horses to the barn. The first was Guinness Stout. A dun chunk of a horse, Guinness came to me young and not very well broken, but he had a heart of gold. I rode him for a year, after which he became Hoot's horse, despite the fact that Guinness bucked him off three times on his first ride. Hoot rode Guinness for more than a decade in Pony Club activities and pair events and took him out with the Golden's Bridge Fox Hunt whenever he was home from school. My good friend Patty Wyman Goodhue also rode Guinness regularly, which he loved because she always came with apples and carrots in her pockets.

Guinness wasn't a playful horse like Slip, nor did he prance like Warlock. He required a lot of "leg" in the ring and strong arms to keep him from munching leaves and grass when we paused on a trail ride. Given a choice, Guinness would probably have spent every day happily eating dandelions in a field. Needless to say, he was always too fat. But he took good care of himself, which meant he took good care of his rider too. I remember one night calling the horses in for supper, but only Slip and Warlock came running. Concerned, I trekked through the pasture, where I could hear Guinness whinnying up the hill in the trees. I found him with a roll of rusty barbed wire wrapped around his legs. I ran for the wire clippers. Smart horse, Guinness never moved and didn't have a scratch when I finally untangled him.

Next into the barn was Patrick, a 17'2" black Irish hunter with huge feet and an ugly head, but also a gentle disposition. Patrick took up residence in a shed adjoining the barn, his large rump providing the chickens and cocks with a warm roosting place during the winter. The product of a divorce, Patrick didn't cost me a penny and for several years took Cindy and various friends foxhunting. He also patiently put up with being dressed up for costume classes at horse shows. Once he was the "elephant" in a safari scenario; another time we entered a Family Class at the Greenwich Horse Show as four "hillbillies" wearing straw hats and bib overalls astride Patrick's broad back. That one required some tough negotiation with Don, who was sure we would humiliate ourselves among all the well-appointed families on their matching mounts. But people laughed with us, not at us, and we won the blue ribbon. Unfortunately, Patrick went lame after just a few years and I had to have him put down.

Woo rode ponies at June and Bunny Broad's stable in North Salem, until Good Time Charlie unexpectedly appeared, soon after I sold Moreland Mousie. I bought him cheap off a guy who, following the birth of his first child, had gotten drunk with his buddies and won Charlie in a poker game. He was quite pleased with the pony, until his wife arrived back from the hospital and gave him an ultimatum: Either that animal goes, or I go! Charlie moved into our barn two days later.

A large strawberry roan pony, Charlie came with lop ears, girth galls and a bald Roman nose. Told that he was a bit "doggy" and needed encouragement, I strapped spurs on Woo (then eleven) and boosted her up. About fifty feet from the barn, he began to crow-hop; after five or six bucks—with Woo's eyes as big as dinner plates—we determined that Charlie did not need spurs. He became a wonderful hunting pony and Woo rode him for years. When Charlie went lame and had to be put down, Woo began to ride Slipstring. She was the only one in the family, other than me, who dared to climb up on him.

Cindy really became a rider on Silver Heels, an old show pony who lived at Eve Whitehouse's barn. Lousy at the hunt but great in the ring, Silver won numerous ribbons at local horse shows. Also, because Silver was almost entirely white, Cindy became expert at grooming and won the stable management award her first year at the annual Pony Club Clinic in South Woodstock, Vermont.

Craigie was still tiny when we arrived in Bedford and bumped along in lead line classes until Sam Savitt gave me Jesse James, a shaggy little spot pony. Unfortunately, he ran off with Craigie at a horse show and that was the end of her riding career. A sturdy beast, Jesse actually rode well with other horses and happily dragged kids on flying saucers through the snow in the winter. He also had no complaints about being dressed up as a "cow" or a "Campbell's soup can" for costume classes and was good with kids at gymkhanas. But he didn't like men and could be quick with a bite or a kick. One summer, when the kids and I were up in Vermont, Jesse nearly ended up at the dog food factory. It seems that Don had gone out to the barn with an apple and Jesse had charged, knocking Don into the mud. That night on the telephone, Don was still swearing "If I'd had a gun I would have shot that damn pony!" Jesse stayed with us until we moved to Denver in 1974, when I put him down.

Foxhunting with the Golden's Bridge Hounds

Don and I joined the Golden's Bridge Hounds (GBH) in 1962 when Dan McKeon and Harry Gibson were joint masters. For the next decade, I hunted Slip regularly during the week; Don joined me on Warlock for weekend meets and the lavish hunt breakfasts that lasted most of the day. I never had an accident and only once did Slip fall with me. It was a cold, snowy day out with GBH, the hounds were running and I had jumped a stone wall with a log rider on top. Slip landed fine, but lost his footing on the steep downhill side. Sitting down on his haunches and with me standing in my stirrups, the two of us tobogganed down that slope at great speed. Neither of us was hurt and we finished the hunt none the worse for wear.

Slipstring, Golden's Bridge Hounds pair event, fall 1964

North Salem was great hunting land; we rode through the woods, up and down ravines, along the sides of farmers' fields, and we had lots of stone walls to jump. Best of all were the friends we made: What a cast of characters! There were the elegant riders like Reggie Fox, Colonel Duncomb and Janet Armour; the unintentionally comic riders, like Diana Westa, who fell off regularly; a few wealthy snobs and the rest of us, who mucked out our own barns and simply loved following the hounds on a bright morning. I became especially fond of Sam Savitt, the well-known horse artist, who enjoyed riding quietly with me at the back of the hunt. When he wrote a book of true horse stories a few years later, he used the story of my great-great-grandfather Dr. Crafts Kimball, whose horse Jenny had brought him safely home one night after a storm had washed out the bridge. Sam did a neat illustration of Jenny with the sleeping doctor, which he gave me after the book was published.

Harry Gibson, a joint master of GBH for many years, became one my best friends in Bedford. Yes, he was a lifelong alcoholic and had a childish sense of humor, but Harry was also exceptionally generous with children who hunted and let me hold Pony Club events on his Running Fox Farm. We had several gymkhanas at his place that I'll never forget.

Our gymkhanas were intended for the entire family. For the kids there were musical chair lead line classes, potato and egg races with a spoon, and balloon-popping dustups. The ladies competed in bareback relay and sack races, but it was the men's events that were most hilarious, not least because many of the fathers had never before been on a horse. Just before the men's apple-bobbing event started, I slipped blue dye into the trough, which of course meant they all came up with blue faces. But best of all was the costume relay. I spent weeks beforehand collecting women's clothes from the Katonah Thrift Shop and neighbors such as Mrs. Lee and Willy Waller, who were happy to dispose of their old-fashioned corsets, which reached nearly to the knee. The old ladies attended and laughed themselves to tears watching grown men struggle with their dresses and undergarments—it made their day.

Harry was often around when I gave the Pony Clubbers lessons; hunting and jumping were fine with him, but he thought dressage was for the birds. One morning when he was coming in from a ride on one of his big hunters, I called Harry over to the ring and asked him to demonstrate how to open and shut a gate. He obliged and then I announced to the kids, "Mr. Gibson has just performed the dressage movement I'm trying to teach you!" Harry was furious that I'd even suggest he was a dressage rider; I teased him about it for years.

Don had a forty-five-minute drive every morning and evening to catch a train to and from New York City. One cold night he came in and said he had a surprise for me: I found one very dead, frozen fox that he had picked up alongside the road stuffed in the car's trunk. I had to laugh; after twenty years of marriage, Don was emulating my mischief. Of course, it wasn't Don who—in the dead of night—took that fox and propped it up, as if driving, in Harry's horse van. I eagerly awaited his telephone call the next morning and wasn't disappointed. Not only had the fox scared him silly, but he had then taken it to the hunt and slipped it into the front seat of the Cadillac belonging to the dour wife of the joint master. There was an uproar, but she could never quite prove who was responsible.

It wasn't hard to persuade Harry to join me in causing confusion. Invited to a big Harvest Fest gala, I had him dress up as a housepainter with a Charlie Chaplin mustache. In he came with his ladder, a big bucket of "paint" and a brush that he

Harry Gibson, joint master, Golden's Bridge Hounds

flourished wildly. While I entertained the crowd, Harry marched throughout the house demonstrating his "painting" skills; it was only later that the guests discovered there had been water and paste in his bucket and he had "painted" all the toilet seats shut!

Hoot worked three or four summers on Harry's farm, and Cindy spent two summers as a "mother's helper" for his and Nora's children. Despite his drinking, he was always a gentleman and a good boss. Harry died just before we left Bedford, and I'll always remember that misty morning at his funeral when Dick Lundy, the GBH huntsman, played "Gone Away" on his horn. I don't cry easily, but I cried.

Animals Inside and Outside the House

Early on in Bedford, Don and I met Fred and Foxie Gwynne through Gracie Huffman, a wild rider and good friend who should have been a professional actress. Fred was an artist and actor in New York City, where he was filming the television series *Car 54 Where Are You*? Foxie was a writer. Enormously bright and full of fun, they invited us to their Easter parties, which were akin to the gymkhanas I put on at Harry Gibson's in terms of craziness.

The Gwynnes had Japanese dachshunds and when the next litter came, they offered us a pup we named Gunther, after Fred's *Car 54* television partner. Bred as a hunting dog, Gunther kept the barn free of rats and could bring down a groundhog with a snap of his jaws. Inside the house, however, he was a wimp. Woo took charge of him, but spent many hours scrubbing a spot at the top of the stairs where Gunther always peed, being too lazy to go outside. He also had a sweet tooth and the kids had to hide their candy carefully or find nothing but tattered bits of wrapper when they came home from school.

After Tucky died and the older kids were away at school, we found a tan and black mutt that Craigie named Muldoon, Fred Gwynne's television persona. A playful dog, he unfortunately didn't understand horses and was kicked in the head. We buried Muldoon in the manure pile.

With only Gunther now left in the house, the kids decided we needed another dog and bought a purebred Airedale from neighbors at the foot of the driveway. Cindy named it Mai-de-Gou—Chinese for "McLeans' Dog"! But what a stupid animal she turned out to be. Maidy didn't like to play outside—the horses chased her, the cats hissed and scratched, and Gunther ignored her when he wasn't eating her kibbles. Maidy spent her entire time sitting on a chair at the dining-room table looking soulfully at me when I was doing my Pony Club paperwork. She lasted about six months before I found an old lady to adopt her. Delighted to be the only animal in a household, Mai-de-Gou lived happily ever after.

Our last dog in Bedford also came from the Gwynnes. After living in California for several years, where Fred was filming the television series *The Munsters* (he was the huge Frankenstein character), he and Foxie returned to build a house just down the road from us. Finished with dachshunds, they now had pugs, and from the next litter came Mugsie, who was a great character and made us all laugh. She and Gunther became fast friends, and both accompanied us to Colorado when we moved in 1974.

As for cats, the Manx we brought up from Kentucky quickly produced Pupdog and Kitcat, and the six-toed Muffy gave birth to several litters of kittens in hard-to-find places in the barn and garage. It wasn't easy to find homes for them all and a few of the cats just disappeared. Craigie was heartbroken when Dirty Snowpants took off, but it wasn't long after that we had a call from St. Matthew's Episcopal Church asking if we owned a big, fluffy gray cat, which had been caught marching across the altar that morning.

Birthday portrait by Fred Gwynne, January 1971

The kids kept white mice and guinea pigs, but more fun were the other outdoor animals—ducks, chickens and fighting cocks. I collected eggs from the horses' feed boxes every morning for breakfast and was reminded of my Watertown buddy Red Hines when the cocks went after each other with their spurs. One of those cocks, however, decided he was king of the castle and seemed to take great glee in chasing the kids. I'd watch them go down the front walk on their way to school, making a huge loop around a small bush where the cock always hid. If they came too close he'd attack. Well, one morning, Don was later than usual leaving for work. I could see tail feathers peeking out from behind the bush and, sure enough, when Don passed, the cock jumped out. But with one swing of Don's briefcase that bird went flying! Chastened, he never ventured outside of the barnyard again.

Golden's Bridge Hounds Pony Club

When we arrived in Bedford in 1961, Dickie Parrish was district commissioner (DC) of the Golden's Bridge Hounds Pony Club. I immediately enrolled the kids, and because Dickie was located near the hunt country, I took over much of the teaching of children in the Bedford area. We did all the usual Pony Club activities—overnight trail rides, gymkhanas, stable management seminars and Know-Downs at my house, after which we'd trek through our back pasture to a dammed-up creek in the woods for a swim. To prepare the Pony Clubbers for foxhunting, I arranged to take them on a "mock hunt" on the trails around Bedford. I told them to bring their own dogs to use as "hounds" to follow a fox scent I'd mail-ordered. The only problem was that the fox scent leaked in the mail, temporarily paralyzing operations at the post office! Dick Lundy, the GBH huntsman, then swapped me the fox scent for some rabbit scent, which didn't stink as badly but which the dogs still recognized. It was a great hunt, with Pony Clubbers on horseback chasing an ecstatic pack of barking dachshunds, terriers, labradors and mutts intent on catching that "rabbit"!

By 1967, Craigie was the only child still at home and my Pony Club involvement began to snowball. I resisted, but found myself agreeing to be co-DC with Harley Kaiser, a Pony Club father; he promised to take care of all the paperwork while I worked with the kids and their ponies. But even with Harley's help, cartons of files and Pony Club manuals began to pile up in the dining room, to Don's chagrin. Later, however, when I became co-regional supervisor with Margo Leithead and was receiving three or four phone calls every night at dinner, Don put his foot down. I think we were the first people in town to install a telephone answering machine. To give him credit, Don was very supportive of Pony Club and always helped out at horse events as an announcer or fence judge.

I really enjoyed working with Margo. Not only did she take care of administration, but she also knew how to look the other way if a kid's heart was in danger of being trampled. I was the examiner for a C-2 rating one summer and one of the Pony Clubbers was an uncoordinated teenager on an uncoordinated mount. Not much of a rider, she had great difficulty performing the tasks required. That horse, however, was beautifully taken care of, her tack was spit and polished, and the teen enthusiastically answered all the questions on the written and oral tests. Since she was going off to college in the fall and I knew she wouldn't continue with Pony Club, I passed her. Margo never said a word and the day ended with a happy child on a happy horse.

On the Trails

In addition to foxhunting and Pony Club, a group of us began a Wednesday morning *ladies' ride*. Gracie Huffman, Marilyn Simpson and Jan Montgomery were just a few who participated, taking turns hosting lunch afterwards. We had some wild rides, but the one I remember best happened down in Katonah's woods. It was early summer, the bugs were already biting and it was blazing hot. We'd ridden several hours and on our way home had to swim the horses across a deep stream. Climbing the opposite bank, we heard splashing behind and turned to find Gracie bare-naked cavorting in the water! I think Jan remembered this episode when, years later, I visited her in California and she suggested a horseback ride along the beach. Off we went, but as we circled some big boulders I nearly ran down a middle-aged man with no clothes on. Shocked, I berated him for his indecency in a public place; he snarled back that I was on a designated nude beach, so what was my problem? Jan just laughed and laughed.

Pony Club event at Gracie Huffman's, 1968

For people with horses, the best aspect of living in Bedford was the extensive trail system, which provided more than one hundred miles of good riding. The Bedford Riding Trail Association maintained the trails, and I spent many hours of many days with my good friend Sue Carter checking for fallen trees, as well as negotiating with homeowners for permission to ride across their land. Most of the trails wound through the woods, but they also intersected with Bedford's many dirt roads. I, therefore, was incensed when I heard rumors that the Bedford town council was planning to turn dirt into asphalt. Rich folks were moving out from New York City and complaining that the dirt roads were bad for their fancy cars. The highways department also claimed that blacktop made the roads easier to maintain in the winter and after heavy rains.

I attended several town meetings to protest, but the officials would neither confirm nor deny the rumors. Then one afternoon I came upon a road crew levelling a section of the Hook Road, in preparation for blacktopping the following morning. Well, I flew home, got on the telephone and by 7:30 the next morning had organized a sit-down strike of a dozen women and children. We plunked ourselves down in front of the bulldozers; the workers just threw their hands in the air and waited for the town supervisor to arrange a truce. The standoff lasted several days, we made the front page of the *Patent Trader* and, despite the threat of a lawsuit, we prevailed. I am happy to say that even in 2004 the Hook Road is still dirt.

Keeping the Hook Road dirt with Patty Goodhue, 1967

In October of 1971, I took Slip out with the Golden's Bridge Hounds for what I assumed would be a gentle hunt through the brilliant fall foliage. We weren't riding hard, but when I popped over a fence, suddenly Slip stumbled and came up lame. I led him back to the trailer and took him home to soak his legs. When he remained lame the next morning, I called my friend and veterinarian Jordan Woodcock to take X rays. After reviewing them, he said he was sad to tell me that Slip's riding days were over.

At 15'2" hands, Slip had always been a rebel—a diamond-in-the-rough kind of horse with choppy gaits, but also great heart and athleticism. For two decades he had dragged us all around on sleds, flying saucers and skis in the winter, and had carried me foxhunting several times a week with GBH. Slip was a great horse and I told him he would always be king of my barn; he could finish out his life munching grass in the pasture. But this wasn't enough for Slip. He began to act up and not so playfully nip me when I took another horse out for a ride. Then one morning, going down the driveway with Guinness and Warlock in the trailer headed for the hunt, I saw Slip in my rearview mirror jump the fence and come hobbling after the car. I had him put down the next day.

Fond Farewells

In 1973, just after Hoot and Susan Gould's wedding in Groton, Massachusetts, and Cindy's return from two years in Taiwan, Don was offered the position of vice president of finance at the Denver Dry Goods in Denver, Colorado. Forced out of Lord & Taylor in 1967 due to computer glitches, he had worked the next seven years for the Gus Meyer stores in New York City. It was a good job, but when Don was invited to return to Associated Dry Goods (which also owned Stewarts and Lord & Taylor) in Denver, we began to pack our bags.

Leaving Bedford Village was not the painful departure that Kentucky had been. Although I had made many good friends and thoroughly enjoyed both Pony Club and the Golden's Bridge Hounds, Bedford was not my cup of tea. An increasingly expensive New York City suburb, it had just too many people with too much money and not enough common sense. Furthermore, new houses were being built on the horse trails, and even the hunt country was disappearing into the hands of developers. I was happy to be heading west—to big skies and open land.

The West

Denver, Colorado
1975–2004

NINE

Restocking the Barn

Colorado was a new beginning. Don flew out first to begin his job; in June I followed with the moving van, and Craigie drove out with Hoot and Cindy. Woo already lived in the state as a student at Colorado State University in Fort Collins.

We rented a place for five months from a retired airline pilot in downtown Denver while we house-hunted. What a disaster! Despite taking them for walks on leashes, Gunther and Mugsie regularly peed in the well-kept backyard, which killed the grass. I was constantly digging up the dead patches and going to the garden store for replacements. Pupdog, clever cat, just roamed the neighborhood in search of birds and was never a problem.

No horses came with us to Colorado. I had put Slipstring down in 1972 after he went lame and, just before we left Bedford, I had put down an aging Warlock. Hoot took Guinness up to New Hampshire. So during the months it took to find a house with a barn, I explored the Denver horse world and kept my eye out for new mounts.

We bought a house on Vista Road, just south of Denver in Cherry Hills. It came with a small barn and pasture on the Highline Canal, the backbone of the Denver

Family reunion, Denver, August 1974

trails network. At that time the area was still largely farmland, many of the roads were dirt, and it was common for people to keep horses behind their houses.

It didn't take long to restock the barn. For myself I found Bridget. She was originally named Baby Bar Doe, but I renamed her Bridget because she was big in the front and big in the back. A registered two-year-old quarter horse, Bridget cost me $200 at a bankruptcy sale up in the mountains. Later I traded Bridget to my horseshoer, Jerry Lay, for lifelong shoeing. Jerry's son rode her to a calf-roping championship and Jerry's wife won ribbons on her in Western Pleasure Horse classes. Sadly, Jerry died young of a heart attack.

For Don I found Woodie, a fifteen-year-old buckskin which, in addition to Robin and Slip, was one of the best horses I ever owned. Formerly ridden by a teenager going off to college, Woodie was just a "good solid citizen" of a horse, and although I had been warned that he didn't like men, he was very good with Don.

And as if we needed more animals, I acquired a baby mule we called Short Snort and was given a supposedly pygmy goat that grew and grew, becoming something of an "attack goat" in the way he could rise on his hind legs and paw the air. We named him Weird Harold.

What was great about Denver was that it was an old cow town, which meant of course an old horse town too. Every January Denver hosted a major stock show, with more than a week of rodeo and horse events accompanying the wheeling and dealing of the cattle barons. The Denver Dry Goods was always a stock show sponsor, which meant Don and I were right in the thick of all the parties and events. It's too bad we didn't move to Denver earlier; I'd have taught the kids to ride Western and might have become a calf roper myself.

Don was so happy to be "back in the saddle" with Associated Dry Goods, where he could drive to his office downtown in half an hour, in contrast to the two-hour commute (each way) he had had when we were in Bedford. He bought himself a little red Mustang and the summer of 1975 built a swimming pool behind the house—a dream he'd had for decades. Once I felt comfortable riding Woodie, I put Don up on him. With me on Bridget, we went out regularly with the Arapahoe Hunt through the winter and fall of 1975.

Don on Woodie, Arapahoe Hunt pair event, October 1975

The morning of November 10, I awoke early and cold. Moving over to warm myself next to Don, I suddenly realized why I was cold: Without moving a muscle, Don had had a massive heart attack in the middle of the night and was gone. He was only fifty-five years old. Lawrence Phipps Jr., master of the Arapahoe Hunt, was kind enough to let me scatter his ashes in a pretty spot on his ranch.

Don's death was a horrible shock; 1976 and 1977 remain a blur for me. Craigie was still in high school and fortunately Hoot was there to help out when I wasn't thinking straight. He and Susan had been living in the apartment attached to the barn, while he gained residency to attend veterinary school at Colorado State. We stayed in the house for the next year and a half while I figured out what to do next.

It was such an unhappy time. After Don's death, Craigie rolled the car over Gunther, who had been sleeping underneath; a marauding dog snatched Pupdog; and Mugsie died of heat prostration the following summer. Only the horses kept me sane.

I didn't know how I was going to pay the bills. Don had been only a few months shy of a pension, but they refused to bend the rules. So I went to work. Bless his soul, the headmaster of Kent School let me pay off Craigie's tuition by giving riding lessons to kids who were required to participate in physical education but had no talent for team sports. I held onto the house until the spring of 1977, then sold it to Dick and Jo Bynny, who came out from California with their three children and a pony. In order to stay close to Kent, I made a deal with them. In exchange for riding lessons, horse and child care, Craigie and I could live in the small barn apartment vacated by Hoot and Susan.

That fall, the Bynnys raised the roof of the barn and added a loft to the apartment; during construction we lived with my good friend Sally Harvey and her family nearby. It turned out to be a good bargain; not only did we have a roof over our heads but Dick, who was a doctor, also stitched me up after several mishaps. We stayed at the Bynnys' until 1986, when Sally built a small cabin on her property and invited Woodie and me to live there. I took care of the barn and introduced her to the Denver horse world on her pony Shadow, in exchange for the cabin and use of her washer and dryer. We spent many hours yakking over coffee in my small, sunny kitchen, when we weren't out riding.

TEN

Pony Club and Coyotes

After I settled in with the Byynys, life took on a pattern that pretty much continued for the next twenty-five years. During the fall and winter, I gave riding lessons, hunted with Arapahoe (and later the Bijou Springs Hunt) and became involved with local pony clubs led by Roe Rodgers, Sylvia MacDonald and Hildy Ritchie. In late spring and throughout the summer, I was on the road as a senior horse management judge for Pony Club rallies and games across the country. Asked to be on the national USPC board, I declined because I couldn't justify the expense and Craigie was still in high school. I also wasn't as interested in the "politics" of Pony Club as I was in working with kids and their animals on the ground.

Hildy—Hildegarde Neill Ritchie—and I became especially good friends. She had been a whipper-in

Hildy Ritchie, Spencer and Roe Rodgers, Pony Club, summer 1977

for the Arapahoe Hunt during the Second World War, when all the men left to go into the service. Later she was instrumental in establishing the Colorado Springs Pony Club, as a district commissioner and regional supervisor for the USPC Rocky Mountain Region.

Hildy's weeklong Pony Club camps were so much fun, always a highlight of the summer for kids and instructors alike. The camps were held on Hildy's property, an old stagecoach stop, where the horses were tied in corrals and fed with hay nets. The routine was to feed the horses, pick up the poops, brush and tack the ponies, and be ready for formal inspection. Then off all twenty or thirty went for a ride, singing songs I made up to familiar tunes like "Over hill, over dale, as we hit the dusty trail, the Pony Club goes riding along!" We played games on horseback in the afternoon, followed by a dip in the swimming pool, where I showed off my "fancy-diving" skills with flips and twists. The day concluded with dinner and lectures by vets and horseshoers on horse care.

The only accident we ever had was when a horse kicked one of the teenagers, breaking her leg. I struggled a slat off a fence and bound her leg to it with a bandage from one of the kids' horses. The doctor who saw her in the emergency room was impressed—I guess I remembered something from my nurse's aide training as a teenager in Watertown.

I also was the examiner for countless D and C ratings. I stayed with the little ones, because I was more interested in seeing kids develop a life-long love of horses than I was in seeing them win prizes at big horse shows and equestrian events. Years ago, I wrote a letter to the *Chronicle of the Horse,* which was printed in the May 21, 1976, issue:

> One takes pride in a well-decorated Christmas tree. The star at the top is breath-taking, but the real beauty of the creation is on the lower branches, where you must do a sensational job, because many more ornaments must be placed on these lower branches.
>
> The same thing happens in the Pony Club. The lowest, biggest branches are your D's, then C's and B's, up to the tip-top A. Like the Christmas tree, the hardest, most important part is the lower portion of the tree, because the star at the top takes care of itself. So, Pony Club workers, stand back and take pride in what you have done, and good luck from a Pony Club worker of twenty years!

USPC rally, Texas, 1975

Teaching kids to be mentors for the little ones was also important to me. My mentors had given me love, respect and discipline, were always fair, and motivated me to achieve what I didn't think I could. I wanted to foster in the kids a desire to contribute something tangible to people less fortunate than themselves. Their reward would be a thanks, a smile and a deep, wonderful sense of satisfaction. Furthermore they would learn leadership skills, useful in their lives as adults.

In the many Pony Clubs I was associated with, we had the kids elect their own officers, put on their own shows and be responsible for thinking up fun activities that everyone could participate in. Adults were available primarily for advice and to ensure safety. Older children became Big Brothers and Big Sisters for the younger ones, teaching them sportsmanship as well as the intricacies of bandaging a leg or braiding a tail. I told them that to be a good mentor required following a few simple rules:

1. Be friendly, but demand respect.
2. Listen to the kids' ideas and respect their thoughts.
3. Have a sense of humor and make the lessons lively.
4. Always be prepared and arrive ahead of time for a class.
5. Be able to admit when you're wrong or have made a mistake.
6. Don't play favorites. Remember that each child and each horse is unique and will learn in different ways.
7. If you don't know something, ask someone who does.
8. If you think a child needs special help or a situation needs changing, be an advocate and speak up.
9. Teach the kids to put their ponies' welfare ahead of their own.
10. Show the little ones how you can ride safely but still have fun.

Over the years, I had several Pony Clubbers who never became very accomplished riders, but were super mentors and instructors of younger children. One little girl, who wasn't even a C, became my chief assistant. I could turn her loose with the Ds and never worry. They loved her for her patience and fairness to all.

Rallies, Games and Stable Management

In between Hildy's Pony Club camp and overnight rides in the mountains, organized by Roe, I crisscrossed the country every summer as a USPC horse management judge from the 1970s through the late 1990s. Frankly, the rallies are a blur for me now, but I always came home with great stories. One rally really sticks in my mind; I think it was in Oregon, where the kids tethered their horses to trees and we all slept in tents. It rained heavily the first day, and in the evening the DC went home for a hot shower, after cancelling a promised swim for the kids. Since they had nothing to do, I gave the kids permission to have a water fight up the hill near the tents until 9:00 p.m., when we all had to go to bed. Around eight, my assistant said she was tired and, despite my warning, trudged up the hill to the tents. The kids caught her

USPC chief horse management judge, Northwest Region

in the port-o-potty, which they promptly tipped over. She wasn't at all hurt, but our tent sure smelled that night.

I came home from another rally with broken ribs. The kids were all roughhousing and my good friend Brad Gordon, who was helping out with horse management, had tossed me into a shallow pond. I didn't hold it against him. I had been egging them all on and he probably just forgot that I wasn't a kid too.

Spending the summers outdoors having fun with kids on their ponies was a true joy. I made so many friends and we had very few problems. Once, at a rally hosted on convent property, the horse trailers left behind deep ruts in one of the fields after a heavy rain. The nuns were hopping mad and threatening to sue for damages, but I calmed them down after promising that we would have a tractor level the ground and mulch it with a truckload of fresh horse manure.

Chasing Coyotes with the Arapahoe and Bijou Springs

Don and I joined the Arapahoe Hunt as soon as we arrived in Denver. Lawrence Phipps Jr.—better known as Lawrie—was the owner of Highlands Ranch and master of the Arapahoe Hunt. If you truly enjoyed watching his hounds work and followed the rules, he didn't care how much money you had or what breed of horse you rode. He only wished for you to join in and have a love for his sport. He was a true gentleman.

Neither refinement nor breeding, but soundness, boldness, common sense, endurance and sure-footedness were his criteria for a good hunter. He welcomed a waitress on her walking horse and didn't require the kids who came out on Saturdays to be "properly attired" in expensive riding clothes. He extended this privilege to me, so when a man in a top hat snidely asked why I was wearing jodhpurs, I told him that Mr. Phipps allowed children up to eighteen to wear jodhpurs . . . and I was in my second childhood!

I had hunted fox up and down the East Coast all my life, but never coyotes! George Beeman was Arapahoe's huntsman and I must say the greatest of all the huntsmen I ever rode behind. When his wife Marguerite stopped riding, she took guests "hill-topping" in her vehicle. I swear, if she could have taught that car to jump, she would have been the first there when they put a coyote to ground. Playing the piano during hunt breakfasts at the Caboose (Arapahoe's clubhouse) was her next love.

George Beeman, Arapahoe Hunt huntsman, 1930–1980

Roe, Sylvia, Hildy and I regularly took the Pony Clubbers out Saturdays, when Mr. Phipps let them ride up front. Roe often spoke about how fun it had been in the 1950s and 1960s to ride from a still-rural Littleton and leave the horses overnight at the kennels. One Saturday we had seventy-one children from all over the area. The only thing we made them do was leave all whips and spurs behind. All came home safely, with big smiles on their faces. The kids never had an accident; it was their instructors who occasionally were run off with or hit the ground with a thud.

The land was fun to ride, full of deep arroyos, gullies and scrub oak as well as flat cattle country. Every hunt was different and we often had seven- to ten-mile runs since coyotes, unlike foxes, don't usually go to ground. Snow didn't bother either Mr. Phipps or George Beeman. We were told that if we lost the hunt in a blizzard, we should just follow the power lines back to the kennels.

Years later, at the new location of the Arapahoe (an old bombing range), Sylvia and I organized a rabbit hunt with beagles for the kids. I rode Sylvia's old horse Amy and because her horse was acting up, we returned to the trailer early. Suddenly the rabbit being chased topped the hill and ran under Amy, who proceeded to stomp on it. With beagles and children coming up fast, I threw the now very dead rabbit over the fence. The beagles grabbed it and everyone thought they'd had a proper "kill"!

I love foxhunting, not for the speed as much as for the sport, the camaraderie and just being in the great outdoors. Consequently, I tended to ride in the back at a slower pace with the timid and the novice, picking up riders who fell off. Woodie was great about letting fallen riders climb up behind my saddle while we chased down the loose horse. One morning, however, a man—who probably shouldn't have even been out at the hunt—managed to fall off three times. Woodie dutifully carried him once, twice, but after the third fall his ears went back as the man approached, so I persuaded him to walk back to his trailer, which wasn't far off.

Another time I followed a gentleman over a fence, then saw him lose both a stirrup and his balance. Woodie and I followed on his heels; galloping alongside I was able to grab his coattail and jerk him back into his saddle. I made a friend for life with that rescue.

The world of foxhunting is really quite small, so I frequently ran into friends of friends at the hunt. One day someone told me a member had brought a guest named Grosvenor Merle-Smith. I galloped up to inquire and, sure enough, met the son of Pat Merle-Smith, whom I'd first met in the early 1940s at Madison Barracks near Watertown. He not only was the aide who accompanied General Patton when he told me my mother had been killed in 1945, but also worked with Miss Charlotte at Foxcroft after the war.

Riding Woodie (right) with the Arapahoe Hunt

One final memory I will always have from the old Arapahoe Hunt is a coyote named Maria. (George named several coyotes that always showed us a good time over the years.) Maria would sit on higher ground while the hounds and field passed below. When they missed her scent, she would howl and then lead them on a merry chase. At the same time, she taught her babies how to elude the hounds.

ELEVEN

Teaching and Other Western Adventures

The porcupine hunter with Caroline Haig's Gretel

The person who really introduced me to the West and western ways was Caroline Haig, a nurse who rode on Highlands Ranch. Mr. Phipps gave her a horse and a six-shooter (vintage 1895, I think) and sent her out with her trusty German shepherd to dispatch porcupines, which sent quills into the noses of "snoopy" horses and hounds. (Afterwards she sold the quills to the Indians, who used them to decorate moccasins.) I rode with her during the summers and in the fall when there was no hunt. She taught me the territory, which included Tweet Kimball's Cherokee Ranch and other smaller landholdings. On occasion, we scared off trespassers and poachers too. Yes, we were a tough-looking twosome—she with her pistol on her hip and me with a rifle under my saddle! She also showed me where the best raspberries, blackberries and asparagus grew; where to find petrified wood, Indian petroglyphs and . . . snakes! I had great fun passing on all this lore to Pony Clubbers and any adults at the back of the hunt who were similarly snoopy. Before Caroline went to a "better place" in 1977, she gave me her great hunting dog, Gretel.

Life in Denver wasn't entirely about horses, Pony Club and coyote hunting. Fascinated by the mountains and land, I took a geology course at the University of Denver, which convinced me that there was still gold to be found in "dem dar hills." For many years I continued with the Junior League and thoroughly enjoyed our "Over the Hump" group, which gamely followed me into the mountains to explore ghost towns, peer down old mine shafts and look for dinosaur tracks. When the grandkids came along, I taught them to pan for gold too. With a little "salting" of the creek bed beforehand, they always came up with a nugget.

When we lived on Vista Road, I became intrigued with the goings-on over the fence at Marvin Davis's estate. Marvin was a western character of a different sort—a land developer who struck it rich turning good ranchland into subdivisions with monster homes. He was also a major supporter of Republican politicians and periodically had big parties under tents set up on his lawn. He brought his important guests in by helicopter; former secretary of state Henry Kissinger was a speaker at one of his soirees. Mucking out the barn, I listened to his speech and at the end shouted, "Mr. Kissinger, I agree with everything you said!" Following a dead silence, he shouted back, "Whoever you are, thank you!"

One Halloween, curious to see the inside of the Davis house, I dressed up as a little ghost and had my daughter-in-law lead me up to the front door with a trick or treat bag. She rang the bell and, after a very long time, a houseman finally appeared. Leaving us on the front stoop, he disappeared, returning with one very small lollipop to drop in my bag. He then asked Susan how old I was and when she told him nine years old, he scolded her roundly for having a child out so late at night.

Living next door to Marvin Davis wasn't all fun and games. I spent one night on the barn roof watching his pool cabana burn to the ground and the bubble over his tennis court collapse. And one afternoon, Craigie's new dog Cirque didn't come home with Gretel. We searched for several days until one morning I found his body in a heap on our side of the fence. The veterinarian said he had died from a whack to the back of the head. I guess the dogs had been trespassing.

National Western Stock Show, 1988

Gretel was a great dog but very protective and she intimidated even Craigie, who stepped carefully around her when I wasn't at home. I really appreciated her talents as a guard dog, however, when my old friends from Kentucky—Nola Wolpert and Carol Thoke—came out for a visit. We took Gretel with us on a road trip up to Montana, where Carol had long-lost relatives related to the Western artist Charles Russell. On the way back to Denver, we stopped for dinner, parking behind an old pub. When we left, I noticed two shifty-looking guys get up from their table and follow us out. My antennae up, I watched them splitting up to corner Carol, who was carrying a big purse.

Making a dash for the car, I threw the door open and "sic'ed" Gretel on them. They split!

I really enjoyed working with Lib Matsch, Brenda Vertmuller, Mary Woolverton and Jan Conant for Riding for the Handicapped. Woo had worked with Lida McGowan in the early 1970s, soon after Lida had set up one of the first handicapped riding programs in the country. Some of the kids were autistic; some had Down's syndrome; some had cerebral palsy and other physical ailments. Tied to the horse, each rider was assisted by three aides—one in front and one on each side—who guided the horse around the ring. We played games all the children could participate in: popping balloons, letting their horses bob for apples in a child's play pool, maneuvering around obstacles, and musical chairs, which in this case were grain sacks on the ground. The kids had a great time and always came supplied with sugar and carrot treats for their mounts. In the end, however, I think the parents benefited even more by seeing their children, with such severe limitations, laughing and interacting with others. Working with horses has a tremendous power to heal.

At some point in the 1980s, I met Cee Wolf, a Denver old-timer who owned a gaggle of dogs, mules, miniature horses and other assorted animals. She lent me Mavis, one of her nicer mules, and we had great fun riding together in competitive 50- and 75-mile endurance events. A wonderful animal, Mavis had only fault: She feared men. During one of our endurance rides, the judge made it clear he preferred Arabs and thought mules shouldn't be permitted to compete. All was well until, during the lunch break, a friend came charging up to tell me Mavis had just gone out of her way to kick the judge.

Cee and I also enjoyed taking the mules for treks in the foothills, where we found dinosaur prints and Indian relics. At this point I was in my seventies and Cee was in her eighties. Our friends all laughed at us because neither of us was more than five feet tall; if Cee fell off, she couldn't get back on her mule, and if I got off to give her a boost, I couldn't climb back on Mavis! I wish I had bought Mavis from Cee when she offered to give me a "deal." But, as Cee was quite the wheeler-dealer, her "deal" probably would have cost me an arm and a leg.

Pike's Peak endurance ride with Mavis, circa 1987

Woo's big, gray "killer cat"—the Wimp—came to live with me when I was living at Sally Harvey's in the late 1980s. Woo was moving to teach at the top of Alaska and felt it unfair to expect Wimpie to adjust to being an indoor cat. So I fixed up a ramp to one of the living-room windows, leaving it open a crack so that he could come and go as he pleased. Wimpie had always been a fearless hunter, and I laughed watching him chase a fox down the driveway. He knew his limits, however, and one night I heard a clatter and arrived to see the Wimp dash through the window with a huge racoon at his heels.

I came home one rainy evening and found Wimpie crouched on the floor with a beady eye aimed at the top of the refrigerator. Looking up, I discovered a bedraggled carrier pigeon that had become lost during a race and landed at my place. Checking the band on its leg, I called the owner and sent it home the next day. I think Wimp never forgave me for denying him warm bird meat that should have been his.

Wimpie was smart enough to leave skunks to the neighbor's dog, which always seemed to stink. Hearing loud barking one night, I chased the dog away from a skunk he had cornered, only to have the skunk back towards me with its tail up! Fortunately, it had used up its spray on the dog so I didn't have to bathe in tomato juice for the next week.

After I had Gretel put down, my good friends Charles and Wendy gave me a pup I named Gizmo. A playful beast, he loved to chew on people's shoelaces. Unfortunately and despite my warnings, however, an irresponsible neighbor continued to let Gizmo accompany her on walks. One afternoon, on the Highline Canal, a jogger ran by and Gizmo went for his feet (shoelaces). Scared silly, the jogger threatened to sue me for this "attack," and although I calmed him down, I realized that I couldn't control Gizmo's wanderings and had to have him destroyed.

This was the fall of 1990. It is said that bad things often come in threes. Early December, I went out to feed the horses and found Woodie leaning against a wall. He wasn't eating and hung his head as if in pain. I called the veterinarian and a young intern came over to check him out. It appeared that Woodie had somehow twisted his gut and at age thirty-two was unlikely to get better. I rejected the suggestion of an operation and, with enormous sadness, let the vet put him down.

It was then that Sally told me that she and Bill had decided to move to San Diego, California, to be close to their daughter and grandchildren. Suddenly, at age seventy, I was without not only my dog and horse, but also my home.

Once again, all my belongings went into storage; Wimpie and I had to find a new place to live. Roe Rodgers gave me space in her basement for two years and then, at the kids' insistence, I bought a small bungalow on South Clarkson Street in Englewood. It was just down the road from Maud Duke's, where I kept new horses with her donkey Rosie; the Village Club, where I taught riding; and friends whose animals I tended when they were out of town.

TWELVE

Granny's Insanity and Concluding Thoughts

After Woodie's death in late 1990, I rode a variety of horses given or loaned to me. Kiowa was a gentle Appaloosa but was blind in one eye and I gave her back. Woodie II was a buckskin and looked like my old Woodie, but was crazy and didn't stay long. It wasn't until 1998 that my last pony, Granny's Insanity, arrived at Maud's barn.

Hoot was stationed at this time with the U.S. Army outside of San Antonio, Texas. He was the only one of my kids who still had horses and I always enjoyed visiting with him, Susan and the boys. For Christmas one year, they gave me lessons with a professional who trained cutting horses for cattlemen. I was pretty good—oh, to be young again!

It was during one of my last visits, before they moved to Boiling Springs, Pennsylvania, that I was introduced to a young fiord pony owned by one of their friends. Fiords have become "trendy" animals in the last decade, but I fell in love with him because he looked like his ancestors—Mongolian ponies—that used to roam the

Kiowa, 1992

northern steppes of China. Furthermore, although he was primarily buckskin, he had stripes on his legs and a mane that stood straight up, like a zebra's. Susan noted my enthusiasm and, without much difficulty, persuaded me that I should take him home with me. Named Granny's Insanity by the grandkids—Sandy for short—he arrived in Denver several weeks later.

1998 was a great year. I had my own horse to play with, in addition to Pony Club, hunting activities and a host of horse events, which kept me busy. In late June, I flew up to Woo's place in Alaska, where all the kids and grandkids met for our biannual family reunion and to send Cindy off to work with a British outfit in China. Everyone seemed to be flourishing.

Family reunion, Alaska, July 1998

The Big Dump

Since childhood, I've been able to do all kinds of tricks on my ponies and horses: ride them backwards, stand up in the saddle, or swing down for a stirrup cup. I guess this kind of behavior became second nature, because I didn't think twice when the Hispanic man came up to Sandy with his map, asking for directions. I leaned over to show him where he was on the map, when Sandy suddenly jerked back and away. I came off and landed hard, smashing both my left ankle and elbow. I didn't realize this, however, until hours later when a friend who had been riding with me that morning insisted that I go for X rays. I ended up in Swedish Hospital for about ten days, where they operated on both elbow and ankle. The pain was bad and—preferring to curse than to cry—I know the nurses and other patients were happy to see me go home.

Frankly, I wish I'd been killed. In September 1999, I was seventy-eight but still fit—hunting and teaching and traveling for Pony Club rallies. The kids were grown and well launched in their lives. I had always imagined myself breaking my neck in the hunt field—Gone Away!—and found myself envious of Don, who had died peacefully in his sleep.

Recovery was long and slow, but I announced to one and all that I was *not* retired. Even before I was back on my feet, the kids were taking me in a wheelchair to the hunt to hand out stirrup cups to the riders.

Laid up, I had more time to ruminate on the horse world and Pony Club. I was beginning to feel like an endangered species with my focus on kids having fun with their ponies. With the development of Denver, there were fewer and fewer backyard barns, less and less land to gallop across. Increasingly, Pony Clubbers were riding only in a ring and

Granny's Insanity (Sandy), Christmas 1998

the historic link to fox/coyote hunting was disappearing. Parents were paying thousands of dollars to buy their kids fancy horses and equipment, which shut out children from less wealthy families. And, sad to say, without the opportunity to whoop it up a bit, the boys largely dropped out. This was a pity, because in earlier years some of the boys had gone on to become Olympic champions with their horses.

I also found the growing bureaucracy and multiplication of rules in Pony Club discouraging. Too many inexperienced stable management judges couldn't tell the kids the reasons for some rules, yet applied them rigidly. No common sense. At one rally, a little boy came to me upset that his horse was rubbing his head raw due to the halter all horses were meant to wear in their stalls, in case of a fire. I checked it out and gave him permission to hang the halter right outside the stall. I also left a note for the judge telling her what I'd done, but she had a hissy fit when she found out and penalized his team.

Another time, I was at the warm-up gate, holding kids back until their numbers were called. A little girl, on a horse that was going in circles, became confused and jumped the warm-up fence backwards (with the red flag on the left rather than the right). She hadn't interfered with any of the other children, so I called her back, gave her a warning and let her start over again. The judge later chewed me out for not immediately eliminating her. Come on! Pony Club is not the Olympics and is supposed to be fun.

Once I felt better and could get around again under my own steam, I abandoned my grumblings and returned to Pony Club and coyotes, figuring there were still ways to have fun and make mischief. I formally retired from Pony Club in 2002.

Although the kids insisted that I needed another animal in the house, I resisted. The fenced-in backyard was so small and I wasn't up to walking a dog. The summer of 2001, however, Caroline went on vacation leaving Molly, her Labrador retriever, with me for a few weeks. Weeks turned into months and Molly became my buddy, riding shotgun in the front seat and accompanying me on my rounds when I took care of other people's animals. She slept just outside my bedroom door and was a great watchdog too. I took her everywhere, including down to Mary Ellen Lesage's new ranch and on to Santa Fe the following summer. Early in 2003, however, I noticed she was having trouble jumping into my truck and seemed to be going blind. The vet later told me he suspected Molly had had a series of small strokes. She probably could have limped around for another few years, but she could no longer chase the magpies in Maud Duke's back pasture or play ball. So with a heavy heart, I fed her a last treat and held her in my arms while the vet put her down.

USPC Games Rally, 2002

Concluding Thoughts

As I said at the beginning of *A Life on Horseback*, at eighty-three, I'm about ready to wrap it up and say my farewells. I have been extraordinarily blessed throughout my life with people and horses who supported and loved me in all my endeavors and mischief.

Although Don, the kids and the grandkids haven't been mentioned much in these stories, I trust they know how much I love them and how proud I am of each for the lives they have created. I did the best I knew how and believe I succeeded in teaching them all to be honest, good-hearted, hard-working human beings who also know how to have fun.

Working on this collection of my horse and people stories, I have begun to understand my life and now realize it is exactly like the life of my favorite horse Slipstring. The only difference between us is I am human, two-legged and can speak; Slip was four-legged, an animal and couldn't speak. Even so, we understood each other totally.

Slipstring turned out to be my best friend (after my dear husband Don). I would go to his stall to cry when things weren't going well; he would lie down beside me and seemed to sympathize with my tears. I was a character, full of life, honest (but you had to catch me first), and I loved to cause trouble if I didn't hurt anyone. Slip was exactly the same.

Slip was a small bay horse about 15 hands; never had hind shoes on his whole life. He was full of fun—several times he took his pasture mates on trips over fences at night to friends' houses miles away. He did everything I wanted him to do and seemed to enjoy it all. He drove, he jumped, he hunted foxes, won point-to-points, loved to be dressed up for costume classes and pulled people around in the snow on flying saucers and skis. Afraid of nothing, never sick, never unsound—Slip did it all!

When Slip's legs gave out in 1972, he was only twenty and I promised him he could enjoy retirement and do what he most liked—eat! But he began to show his feelings; increasingly grumpy, he tried to bite if I took another horse out. The morning he jumped a three-and-a-half-foot board fence and came limping after the trailer, I knew the end had come. I turned around, loaded Slip into the trailer and headed out to the hunt, where he was put down. I cried losing my best friend, but he had let me know that seeing as he couldn't do what he wanted to do, it was best to say good-bye. When I go, I expect he will be there to cheer me on.

Slipstring the rogue

I'm nearly at that time myself—I've had a super life and feel that besides being naughty, I've helped people, kids and animals to be their best. It's getting so I can't do what I still want to do and it's making me very cranky. I only wish that we could be as honest in putting people down as we can be with our animal friends. I want to continue to help others and not end up in a care home or hospital, being only a costly burden. Slip let me know in his own way that he didn't wish to live like a vegetable—me too!

My only fear about dying is the fight and stampede that may ensue when I get up to the Pearly Gates. Robin, Slipstring and Woodie will all be waiting impatiently for me. Each was once king of the barn, and I could never really choose one over the other. It will be a trick to figure out how to live together peaceably, but I look forward to riding them all again across the heavens to eternity.

August 2004

As I sit here talking on the telephone, with Cynthia pestering me for more details about Pony Club, I can see a robin trying to haul a huge worm across the grass. Ooops! She's lost it; the worm has disappeared back into its hole. But the robin's not giving up and is pecking at the hole where the worm disappeared. Hurray, she's got it again—probably taking it home for her babies.

It's been a good several weeks, although I sure wish we'd get some rain in Denver. This drought has gone on now for close to five years and the trees are dying. That's one reason I so enjoy taking care of the donkeys at the Taylors'. Their pond provides water for lots of wildlife and, with the crackdown on coyotes and fox by Greenwood Village, the rabbit population has skyrocketed. They are everywhere and the hawks know it too. I've watched those big birds soar over the pastures and then suddenly swoop to the ground, coming away with a baby rabbit in their talons. It's sad, of course, for the rabbits, but that mother hawk probably has babies to feed too.

I spent last weekend in the Black Forest, just north of Colorado Springs, directing horses and riders to the jumping ring and cross-country course. It rained heavily and we had to move the practice jump several times, because the footing became so mucky. I told the riders to take it slow; getting around safely was more important than a fast time. I guess they listened, because there were no injuries and everyone seemed to have a good, if soggy, day.

Two weeks ago, I helped out an old Pony Clubber at her three-phase event. Her son has a paint pony with white spots that are hard to keep clean. I suggested that brown or black men's hair dye would do away with those troublesome spots. He giggled, but his mother looked horrified.

Yesterday I rode Sue Fitzpatrick's big black horse. Damn, he's learning he can push the "old lady" around! Still, it was nice to be out and see the mountains on horseback. This fall I either will get Sandy going again—ride regularly—or I will find a good home for him. He's only nine and could be a great ride for a child. It's such a waste of a sturdy pony for him to be standing in the field doing nothing but eating grass and getting fatter.

On this note, I will end my saga, which has gone on much too long. There remain many stories yet to be told, but perhaps it is better for others—with more objectivity and better memories—to tell them. In the meantime, there are more horses to ride, more Pony Clubbers to teach, more stirrup cups to hand out at the hunt and more fun to have. Not bad for an old lady of eighty-three, eh?

Starting gate judge

Author's Postscript

On Being My Mother's Daughter

It is December 2004, just days before Christmas. I sit at Mother's table sorting through her Christmas cards. Some of her friends I have known since childhood; others are unknown to me. I look at holiday photos of smiling children; she tells me they are the children of the children of Pony Clubbers she taught many, many years ago. I marvel at the growing stack of warm memories and good wishes—Mother receives more Christmas cards than anyone I've ever known. She's nearly eighty-four years old and most of her peers have died, but the cards flow in. The youngest friend so far is eight, a little girl in a photograph flying over a jump on her pony. Mother was the examiner who granted her a D-1 Pony Club rating last fall.

Of course, Mother doesn't just receive cards, but sends them too. Every year since Daddy died in 1975, she has used Christmas to keep in touch with her far-flung network. With great forethought, she thinks up an outrageous scenario involving herself and one of her animals, usually a horse. The laugh-out-loud photo is then sent in the New Year, with a personal note and greetings. The cards are eagerly awaited. One of her friends has a near-complete file of Mother's cards; others post them on refrigerator doors. She's still ruminating on her 2005 scenario and has given no hint of outcome. I too must wait to be surprised and amused.

The Molly Maid having fallen through (my Christmas gift to Mother), I proceed to dust and sweep and polish up her house. It is a Zen-like exercise that gives me the opportunity to revisit Mother's life, through the minutiae that carry so many memories. To clean the long wooden bench in the living room, I first remove a pile of her Pony Club and horse-event caps to the hat rack in the study. The hat rack groans as I pile on caps inscribed with *Golden's Bridge Hounds, Rio Grande Region, USPC Nationals—The Indian, Bijou Springs Hunt, Horse Mgmt, State Games Colorado, Plum Creek Hollow, Black Canyon Pony Club, North American Young Riders' Championships, Village Club Cherry Hills* and *Special Olympics World Games 1995.* Her favorites are *Woodie* (her last beloved horse) and *Genuine Antique Person.* There are more than I can count and I stack them up three and four deep.

Spencer in Woodie cap

To dust table surfaces, I rearrange Mother's numerous awards. There is the cast-iron sculpture of a small woman on a small horse, both gazing down at hounds underfoot. The inscription reads *The Arapahoe Hunt Honors Spencer Kimball McLean, 1995.* On the bookshelf in the study is a silver handheld bullhorn: *Spencer McLean: In Appreciation, Centennial Pony Club.* Next to the bullhorn is the English hunting horn that Dinwiddie Lampton, master of the Oldham County Hounds, gave her in 1961.

Back in the living room is another sculpture, of a horse nibbling its rider's shirtsleeve: *Spencer McLean—In Appreciation for your years of support to foxhunting, youth and equestrian sports in Colorado. The Bijou Springs Hunt. The Mitchell Family.* Crammed into a corner cupboard are two large silver trays. One reads *Presented to Spencer K. McLean, District Commissioner, Golden's Bridge Hounds Pony Club 1967–1970, In Grateful Appreciation for Devoted Leadership.* The other reads *USPC Founders Award 1993 Spencer K. McLean.* I have a 1961 newspaper clipping that shows Mother receiving yet another silver plate, in appreciation for her work in establishing the Anchorage chapter of the Blue Grass Pony Club, but that plate is nowhere to be found. Finally I find *Chatham Hall 1940 Spencer Kimball* on a small silver cup. Chosen as the student most embodying the spirit of Chatham that year, Mother is proudest that the cup proves she graduated from high school.

Then there are her various riding trophies to sort and polish: *Cold Creek Riding Club Handy Hunter 1938, Cornell Horse Show 1935 Novice Jumping, Madison Barracks 1934* and—my favorite—*Jefferson County Riding Club 1929 Best Rider 6–10 Years Old.* These are but a few of the dozens of silver trophies that lined the bookshelves of every house we lived in.

I move into the bathroom to clean the windows and laugh again at the painting of Mother astride a leaping zebra. The artist and actor Fred Gwynne created it for her fiftieth birthday; one of her few unfulfilled dreams is to ride a zebra to the hunt. As a child attending the circus, she had seen a man jump a zebra over a car, so she dismisses as rubbish the notion that zebras are impossible to train to saddle. She came close to acquiring her zebra in the 1960s, when a private zoo closed down, but Daddy determined we had enough animals and the barn was full. The zebra dream, however, is well known to her friends and the house is full of zebra prints, glasses, wooden sculptures, napkins and ceramic striped beasts of all sizes. Mother's favorite Christmas gift this year was a zebra hat with floppy ears and a long tail. She wore it to the Bijou Springs Boxing Day hunt, where—as is her custom—she handed out stirrup cups of port to the mounted riders.

Valentine's Day at the Arapahoe Hunt with Lawrence Phipps III

The zebra hat is merely one more addition to Mother's costume collection. Stored in a big box at the bottom of her closet are the red long johns that transform her into Cupid for Valentine's Day, and the green sweaters and hats that make up her leprechaun outfit on St. Patrick's Day. Her Halloween witch costume, worn to a hunt twenty years ago, exists only in a photograph, as do other award-winning costumes she created for horse show costume classes and gymkhanas. More ephemeral, but critical to Mother's theatrical talents, is a repertoire of songs—mostly bawdy—which with very little encouragement she has sung for years at hunt breakfasts and dinner parties. She misses the Caboose at the old Arapahoe Hunt, where Marguerite Beeman would accompany her on the piano. Mother is a born entertainer. The horoscope for the date of her birth states that persons born under her sign make good actors; she is certain that her next lifetime will be played out on the stage.

I tire of dusting and polishing. Mother tires of watching me dust and polish. So we prepare for the Sunday hunt—one of three that I catch during my visit. The first is a joint Bijou Springs–Arapahoe Hunt, with Bijou as host, off Happy Canyon Road just east of I-25. The morning is sunny but cold; Mother and I hand out stirrup cups of port, wandering around horses and riders in various stages of dress. Some I recognize from a Bijou event last fall; most are new faces with names I've heard from Mother over the years. The hounds pile out of their trailer baying and milling about as the huntsman herds them towards the gate. In short order the field is gone, pink coats and red-ribboned tails disappearing over the first rise. Following the "chase" is a hunt breakfast at a lovely home up the hill. Mother chats and entertains a crowd, pretending (since she refuses to upgrade her hearing aids) she can hear responses in the clatter of dozens of voices.

Arapahoe hosts the second hunt, across Lawrence Phipps III's ranch some distance away. Lawrence has invited his landowner neighbors to participate, so there are Western saddles, blue jeans and cowboy hats mixed among the well-appointed members of Arapahoe. More children are expected and Mother brings candies rather than port. The hunt departs; we clamber into a four-wheel-drive vehicle with the master's wife and follow on hilltop. The country is full of ravines and arroyos, and we lurch across the fields, watching the coyotes run one way while the hounds go another.

Mother and the master's wife discuss the attributes of different kinds of hounds: Penn Marydels are slower but have better voice; English hounds are faster and have tough feet, better suited to the rocky Colorado land. The hunt breakfast is held in a huge, open tractor shed.

The third hunt belongs to Bijou Springs and is held the day after Christmas in Larkspur. Mother dons her zebra hat and gathers up the port she forbade me to drink the night before. Again we hand out stirrup cups and I am introduced to various Pony Clubbers Mother has taught over the years. I know only a few of the riders, but they all know me when I tell them I am Spencer's daughter. We watch the field depart through a mist that will have evaporated by the time everyone returns for breakfast.

Bijou Springs Boxing Day hunt, December 2004

I myself haven't hunted in years, perhaps since the 1960s when I went out with the Golden's Bridge Hounds in upstate New York. Somewhat to my surprise, I find myself jealous of the riders, telling myself I could hunt for two hours at a trot or gallop, although I've not been on a horse in a very long time. I am reminded of hacking to an early fall hunt with Mother and a gang of kids on ponies. We took off at about four in the morning; the woods were dark, the only light we could see the sparks hit off rocks by the horses' metal shoes. I enjoyed foxhunting and loved the annual landowners' party, where we ate tons of fried chicken and corn-on-the-cob, then square-danced all night surrounded by bales of hay and the farmers' prize corn stalks.

Back at the house, snow has fallen; it is a frigid December day. I resume my Molly Maid endeavors and tackle the bookshelves, crammed with volumes on foxhunting, Pony Club, mules, General Patton, draft horses, riding for the handicapped, eventing, stable management and riding trails around Denver. I pull out Gordon Wright's *Horsemanship and Horse Mastership: The Cavalry Manual of Education of the Rider* and his *Riding Instructors Manual*, illustrated by Mother's good friend Sam Savitt. She credits Gordon Wright as one of her mentors, an instructor who really understood what makes a horse tick and was capable of conveying that to students. She laughs, telling stories of how he used her and Slipstring to demonstrate (or not) how to trot through a cavaletti without stirrups and with arms outspread.

I paw through a box full of stable management materials and Pony Club manuals; the earliest is the fifth annual report, illustrated by her USPC friend and colleague Jan Conant. In 1960, the Pony Club initiation fee is $25 per club and $1.50 per child. Howard Fair is president and Alice Reidy is secretary, with all the national USPC files stacked in her Massachusetts basement. Mother once called Alice for advice and was told, rather sharply, that since Alice did not know the club or the horses or the kids, she had no idea what should be done and that if Mother couldn't figure it out, she'd find someone else who could! Mother figured it out.

According to the report, eighty-one clubs are active in 1960. Miss Hildegard Neill is regional supervisor as well as district commissioner and secretary of the Colorado Springs Pony Club. Mrs. Keith (Sylvia) Robinson is DC and secretary of the Platte Valley Pony Club, territory of the Arapahoe Hunt. Hildy writes: "The highlight of our year was our first inter-club rally with the Platte Valley Club. With almost no budget, every effort was made to follow 'Guide to Rules for Rallies.' Parents, children and friends did all the work from the building of the Cross Country Course, to painting the stadium jumps, making contestants numbers and supplying picnic lunch for the guests." Sylvia writes: "The hunting this fall has been the best ever. The scenting conditions were superb and the fast pack really got us in shape quickly. The children's Saturday meets were everything but mild. One pony took a short cut through the dense scrub oak and his young rider was never unseated, but lost her hat and stirrup. The latter never could be found . . . Our dismounted meetings included movies and a wonderful lecture by our Huntsman, Mr. George Beeman."

USPC fiftieth jubilee legends, January 2004

I then turn to the Kentucky Blue Grass Pony Club, where Jean Gordon and Ruby Rodes are district commissioners. Nancy Lampton, secretary, writes: "All is not work. We had a very successful gymkhana. The groups had picnics, rides and paper chases. This summer the Louisville polo team arranged for the Pony Club to play broomstick polo in the arena between the third and fourth chukkers." Mother organized this event; nine years old at the time, I remember the matches well.

Pony Club was a constant presence in our house throughout my childhood. I only reached C-2 standing, but my sister Woo became an A, pleasing Mother enormously. I stopped riding seriously in high school, but always enjoyed going for a ride when I came home. I knew Mother would never put me up on a horse that I couldn't handle.

Our morning routine, when I am visiting Mother, is to gather some breakfast and sit down with the *Denver Post.* Now that the election is over, I don't curse as much. Still, the brouhaha about the absence of a Christian float in the annual Santa Claus Parade is obnoxious. As a practicing Christian, I really think the Jesus, Mary and Joseph story belongs in churches and not in the public square. I growl at Iraq stories that name every U.S. soldier lost but ignore the thousands of Iraqis who have died. Mother tells me to "get a life" and turns to the sports section.

I follow world politics closely. As a senior in high school I had a choice of Chinese or calculus. I chose Chinese and spent the next thirty years in the China field, fending off American Cold War attitudes and accusations of being a Communist. After two years at university, I went to Taiwan—in 1971, the only "China" open to U.S. students. Not only did Mother support me in this adventure, but she sturdily defended the decision to her friends, who were sure I would be sold into the "white slave trade." When I came home the summer of 1973 for my brother's wedding, she was disappointed that I'd not stayed long enough for her to visit. She'd already lined up a seat on a cargo plane. Years later, when I was working in China, she again was disappointed that I didn't stay long enough for the two of us to explore the Mongolian steppes on horseback.

Mother had no real "China connections," beyond good memories of a Watertown Chinese restaurant that served "flied lice." I think it was her overseas experience with the American Red Cross during World War II that sparked my curiosity about the world outside the United States. She also instilled in us all a keen sense of duty and justice. While definitely ingrained by both her parents, this passion for right and wrong was reinforced when, as an American Red Cross Clubmobiler, she accompanied General Patton to the liberation of Buchenwald in April 1945.

Mother taught us to respect the ditch-digger who did an honest day's work as much as the president. It is a matter of dignity and pride. She walked her talk with Fran Lane, the milkman; Tom and Mary Mason, a black couple in Kentucky; Dominic Vallone, who cleared the Bedford horse trails and invited her every Christmas to sample his homemade wine; and countless other garbage men, horseshoers, mailmen, landowners, grooms, cleaning ladies and workmen who helped her out. She also walked her talk when Daddy died and she had to find a way to support herself and Caroline in 1975. For nearly the last thirty years she has given riding lessons to children and adults, taken care of animals when their owners are away, and found other ways to barter her talents for horses and lodging. At the same time she has continued to give countless volunteer hours for Pony Club and horse events throughout the country. She never complained and remains quite proud that even today she can pay her own way, without going to the bank.

As a child in upstate New York, Mother collected arrowheads and believed that the Indians had been "robbed." She took us as children to dances at the Onondaga Indian Reservation (Iroquois Confederacy) and maintains to this day an interest in Indian affairs, demonstrated by the large number of small Indian charities she supports. I think it is the Plains Indian lifestyle on horseback that most intrigues Mother, including a worldview that finds deity in nature. As she grows older, her weather-beaten face has taken on the look of a native elder. Today in British Columbia—since I decided to go "local," after so many years of being "global"—my writing and teaching focus on Indian residential schools and the recovery of First Nations language and culture.

I never knew a guinea pig could be so entertaining. When Molly died two years ago, Mother steadfastly refused to take in another dog, which would likely outlive her. Unable to imagine Mother without some kind of "creature" in the house, sister Caroline and I plotted. So last August, Caroline arrived from Boulder with her children Eric and Kate in tow, lugging a cage, a ten-pound bag of nibbles and a wee guinea pig, promptly named Brandy for the color of her coat. Mother agreed to keep Brandy for the two weeks they would be in Crested Butte, but even before their return, she began to suspect she'd been snookered.

She protested loudly that Brandy was good only for a coyote snack, but it wasn't long before Mother was out in the yard picking dandelion treats for her "pet." Brandy also quickly learned that when Mother returned from feeding the horses, there was usually fresh hay with tassels to supplement her store-bought diet. Consequently, at the first sound of the car, Brandy now leaps to attention and "speaks" loudly in expectation of fresh goodies. I really knew Mother was hooked, however, when I tried to put Brandy into a harness and take her for a walk on leash this Christmas. After much guinea pig yelling and hollering, Mother marched into the room and snatched Brandy out of my hands, tossing the harness into the trash. Brandy's cage now sits on the dining-room table where Mother writes letters, reads and pays bills.

Dancing at the GBH Hunt Ball, 1969

Still in Molly Maid mode, I close Mother's bedroom door in order to polish the mirror behind it. On the wall hangs a large photograph of Mother with Daddy, taken out at the old Arapahoe kennels just weeks before he died. He is dressed in a business suit; Mother is in her dirty blue jeans. With his arm around her shoulders, Daddy smiles down bemused; she looks up as if she has just told a clever joke. It is such a typical pose and I wonder again how Daddy, who always was immaculately turned out, married Mother, who strenuously resisted dressing up. Worse, she hated to shop. When Daddy was working for Lord & Taylor, she once bought a dress from the thrift store, added Lord & Taylor tags and tried to pass it off as new! In truth, Mother had plenty of clothes in her closet for any occasion, but because she rode nearly every day, she was almost always in jeans. Furthermore, since she was responsible for the care of all the horses and ponies we ever owned, Mother spent much of every day mucking out the barn, carrying buckets of water for the horses in winter, fixing the fences and occasionally shooting a woodchuck in the back pasture. Daddy, I guess, figured it was a fair trade-off. She quotes him as saying "You were often a problem, but never a bore!"

Mother no longer "does Christmas." Undeterred, I set about wrapping presents and gently decorating the living room with strands of fake cranberry and mistletoe. My best idea, however, is to collect the dried pods of the yucca cactus (from Maud Duke's front field) and glitter them gold. In a silver dish, covered with Christmas potpourri, the effect is quite stunning; it looks like Japanese ikebana. Now *this* Mother appreciates. Artistic herself, she was once president of a garden club, where she won awards for her displays of old boots and dried flowers. But she then proceeds to badger me about never publishing *Misery in the Hunt Field*, a collection of cartoons I drew in the 1960s. Based on her stories of misadventures with the Golden's Bridge Hounds, several of the cartoons were published in the *Chronicle of the Horse*, but I was off to Cornell and moving out of the horse world. Years later, Mother used several of my hunting cartoons as Christmas cards.

Conventionally religious, Mother was baptized, confirmed and married in the Episcopal church in Watertown, but the Church has never meant much to her. She told a friend recently that when she was young she did a "stint" as a Christian, but then moved on. Essentially a pagan, Mother has always found God in nature—in animals and streams, in windswept clouds and snowstorms, in the woods and on the land. She has a sharp eye for birds and snakes and coyotes; any time we were near water, she was down at the edge, picking up rocks, looking for crawdads and other creepy crawlies. My marriage, therefore, to a Church of England priest following my degree at Union Theological Seminary in New York City came as something of a shock to her. She only relaxed when she realized that my Christianity was of the Chinese and American Indian varieties.

So on Christmas Eve, while I walked a few blocks through the snow to a Catholic mass, Mother went to bed. But she was terribly disappointed the next morning when I told her that the church had had a living nativity scene with a cow, a pony, several sheep and miniature goats leaping about and butting the angels. Next Christmas maybe she'll join me for church.

We spend Christmas morning with Candy Gray and several of her friends. Mother enjoys Candy's "open door" policy, which means dogs big and small are racing in and out in pursuit of squirrels. Candy is a longtime horse friend who was responsible for giving Mother the supposedly miniature goat that turned into "Weird Harold." Fully grown, Weird Harold towered ten feet on his hind legs and was capable of jumping the corral fence. Mother was also a close friend of Candy's mother, Carol, who not only was her real estate agent when she and Daddy moved to Denver, but also turned out to be a long-lost friend from Camp Fenimore in Cooperstown, New York. Christmas with the Grays always included renditions of Camp Fenimore songs, in two-part harmony. I especially liked Carol, because she grew up in Manhattan and I lived more than a decade in New York City. She and I had conversations impossible to have with Mother.

Christmas breakfast over, we return to the house, unwrap our presents and begin to prepare for the Bijou Springs Hunt the next day in Larkspur.

Post-Christmas, it is getting on time for me to return to Vancouver. Before I leave, however, Mother and I make one last effort to find the road off University Avenue that will take us to Daniels' Park Road, the buffalo herd and Tweet Kimball's castle. The highest rise in Denver, the road offers magnificent views of the valley, most of which belonged to Lawrence Phipps Jr. when Mother and Daddy came west in 1974. Mr. Phipps was then the master of the Arapahoe Hunt, which based its stables and kennels on his 24,000-acre Highlands Ranch. Mother misses riding over this land, which is much more varied than the bombing range where the new Arapahoe now hunts.

The Ghost of Highlands Ranch Past, fall 2000

After Mr. Phipps's death the ranch was sold for development, and the land is now covered with huge houses, endless rows of condominiums and shopping centers. Mother grumbles about the loss of open country and mutters darkly about a cyclone sweeping away all the cheap construction. She also wonders if Daddy's ashes, scattered on Highlands

Ranch in 1975, now lie beneath someone's hot tub. But once we successfully wind in and around the subdivisions and arrive at the peak of Daniels' Park Road, which is still dirt, we become silent. Turning our backs on the ugly development, we gaze towards the mountains where the valley opens up and it is easy to imagine the cattle drives that would have snaked up to Denver before World War II. The land is big, the land is beautiful and Mother is in her element.

Packing my bags, I sense the presence of Carola Kimball, Mother's mother, all around me. My great-grandmother, Carola's mother Ella, presides over the house from a handsome Victorian tintype, in which she is dressed for a ball. Ella's mother was the wife of Gustavus Spencer, who managed a sugar plantation on Maui during the Civil War. As Ella Rosamond, Mother's grandmother became a professional singer on the Philadelphia stage at the turn of the century. Sadly, she died before my Grandmother Carola was six.

I am very aware that I am a part of this procession of mothers' daughters. I recognize that certain traits jump a generation and that, in some ways, I am more like my grandmother or great-grandmother than like my mother. This lets us both off the hook.

After nearly three weeks, I am tired of sleeping on the couch and Mother is tired of watching me clean. She complains that I have become her "babysitter" and I am happy to return home to Canada.

I walk back into my Vancouver apartment on New Year's Day and marvel at the differences in our lives. My many bookshelves are lined with books, not silver trophies, and evidence of my China and First Nations pursuits is everywhere. The only horses in view grace a Nepali card, sent me by my once sister-in-law, and a recent photograph of Mother on Sandy. I hop on the Internet to catch up with my email; I take a walk along the seawall of English Bay and pick up a Starbucks coffee on the way home. I have a presentation to prepare for a discussion group at the cathedral tomorrow morning. Standing on my balcony, I look out over the water and mountains—seeing just how much Mother's love of wilderness led me to put down roots in this beautiful city.

I stop by the drugstore to drop off film containing photographs of what may become Mother's 2005 New Year's card. The only hint I will give is that they include pictures of her fiord pony, Granny's Insanity. Once they're developed, I'll send her the prints. Everyone else will have to wait to be surprised and amused.

On the surface, our worlds are radically dissimilar. I don't own a horse and Mother despairs of my intellectual pursuits ever providing me with a liveable income. But I am very much my mother's daughter. I have been blessed.

Cynthia Kimball McLean
Vancouver, British Columbia
January 2005

Cynthia and Spencer, Sante Fe, 2004

SPENCER'S 2005 NEW YEAR GREETINGS

New Hunt	The Red Hat Hunt We go out 2 times a month.
Members	Women over 75 yrs of age
Horses	Unsound, but still love life
Hounds	2 1/2 couple that can still walk
Happiest Animal	The coyote who is always waiting for us to come out and play with him.

"Oh what a wonderful day!"

Acknowledgments

Thank you brother Hoot and sisters Woo and Caroline
For believing in this book
And supporting its production.

Thank you Chessie TenEyck
And Fred Carter
For being rocks in the storm.

Thank you Robin Pascoe
Brilliant writing coach and stalwart friend
Who harassed me through the writing.
Thank you Naomi Pauls and Patty Osborne
For superb editing and design.

Thank you all of Mother's astonishing friends
Who each caught a glimmer
Of Spencer
Never forgot it and passed it on.

Glimmers of Spencer from her Friends

May the spirit of Spencer run with the wind—like the horses she loved so.

Spencer was a poster child for the saying "Inside every old person is a young person wondering what happened." She was forever young and fun.

I remember Spencer putting my dad in his place (seldom seen event) with her Patton stories. This was my first inkling of true "Girl Power."

I always thought I was funny, until I met Spencer.

Even the hottest horses stood quietly for her while she checked their bits and girths at the starting gate.

With sparkling eyes and a big smile, she had a gift for making children, horses and adults all feel welcomed, comfortable and worthwhile.

Who's going to give us candy now? (D-1)

A face full of life's experiences, Spencer was a real piece of history.

My father, a retired rancher, gave Spencer the ultimate compliment after swapping stories with her. "She's a dyed-in-the-wool cowboy!"

Often I wonder why I chose to ride thousand pound animals. During my ten years of riding horses, I have been scared many times and once actually considered quitting altogether. The summer when I was nine (1991), I fell off my horse as I was jumping a cross rail. Nothing was broken except for my confidence, but the fall prevented me from taking my D-2 rating in Pony Club. I didn't want to jump ever again and was really in a rut. Towards the end of the summer, Spencer McLean, a family friend as well as a U.S. Pony Club National Horse Management Judge, came to Steamboat Springs to help our Pony Club with its annual games day. While staying at our house, Spencer decided I needed a riding lesson. I did not want to jump, but Spencer knew better.

You have to understand what Spencer is made of. She is more than seventy in age, about five feet tall and has wrinkles as deep as canyons from laughing and smiling so much. Take a closer look and you almost see a vivacious twenty-year-old. She speaks with a throaty but not harsh voice and walks with confidence. You can always find her either whistling or singing. She lived through World War II as a Red Cross Clubmobiler and has helped hundreds of kids overcome the obstacles that go with learning to ride. She can light up the face of an eight-year-old as easily as that of an eighty-year-old.

By the end of that evening, Spencer had me jumping. She began by just getting me comfortable again with myself and the horse on the flat, and then she put up a small jump. She took the time to go step by step, so that by the end of that lesson I was jumping without using hands or eyes, something that had seemed impossible just hours earlier.

Spencer has an amazing ability to show others that they are capable of doing anything. It's hard to live without the confidence to be who you are. Spencer illustrates individuality perfectly: Physically she is only five feet tall, but spiritually she is a giant. Best of all she has found a way to help kids like me to recognize strength in ourselves.

—A Pony Clubber's college application essay, 1998

Exercising horses at the hunt

Permissions

Bette Savitt, PO Box 302, North Salem, NY 10560-0302, savitt@optonline.net, for drawing of "Jenny" by Sam Savitt, Chapter 3

Chatham Hall, 800 Chatham Hall Circle, Chatham, VA 24531, www.chathamhall.com, for photo of Miss Virginia Holt, Chapter 4

Charles M. Province, The Patton Society, 3116 Thorn Street, San Diego, CA 92104-4618, www.pattonhq.com, for drawing of and quotes by General George S. Patton Jr., Chapter 5

Books that Provided Inspiration

Bateson, Mary Catherine. *With a Daughter's Eye: A Memoir of Margaret Mead and Gregory Bateson* (W. Morrow & Co., NY, 1984)

Cunningham, Elizabeth. *Small Bird: Poems and Prayers* (Station Hill, Barrytown, NY, 2000)

Estes, Clarissa Pinkola. *Women Who Run with the Wolves: Myths and Stories of the Wild Woman Archetype* (Random House, NY, 1992)

Morgan, Marjorie Lee. *The ARC in the Storm: A Personal History of and by the Clubmobilers in the European Theatre of War during World War II* (Hazlett Printing, St. Petersburg, FLA, 1982)

Morris, Robert R., *The United States Pony Clubs, Inc., A Story to Tell: 1954–2004* (Donning Co. Publishers, Virginia Beach, VA, 2004)

My Friend

You rest now, dear, upon the hill
Where once you cantered free.
For God has made his call on you
And taken you from me.
They say you went the way you came,
Your beauty still unfurled.
And in your eye a fire that spoke
A challenge to the world.
You were a teacher and a friend
In whom I could confide.
My wildest dreams, my hopes, my fears
As while we two would ride.
I love you still, though you are gone,
No other can take your place.
And so in dreams I'll saddle up
And o're the fields we'll race.

—Given to me by Mother in 1938
when I put Robin down

SPENCER KIMBALL McLEAN

January 28, 1921 – May 16, 2005